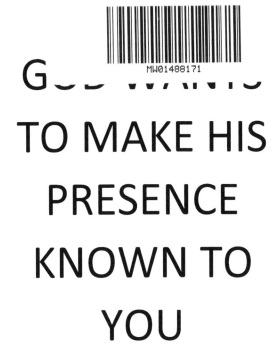

GOD WANTS TO MAKE HIS PRESENCE KNOWN TO YOU

BY: JAMES W. ARMOUR, LAYMAN IN CHRIST

James W. Armour

Table of Contents

WHO CAN ENTER IN THE KINGDOM OF HEAVEN? (CHAPTER 1)

MATTHEW 5:3 Blessed *are* the **poor in spirit:** for theirs is the kingdom of heaven.

ONLY THE **PURE IN SPIRIT** WILL SEE GOD, JESUS WENT AWAY TO PREPARE A PLACE FOR THOSE WHO WOULD BELIEVE IN HIM (JESUS), WHO WOULD KEEP HIS WORD, AND KEEP HIS COMMANDMENTS. HOW CAN WE SAY WE LOVE GOD, AND NOT KEEP HIS COMMANDMENTS? PEOPLE SMILE IN YOUR FACE, EVEN TELL YOU THEY LOVE YOU; TO ONLY STAB YOU IN THE BACK. PEOPLE GO ABOUT THEIR DAILY LIVES NOT KNOWING WHO GOD IS. GOD IS NOT JUST A MAN TO BE PLAYED WITH, GOD IS A SPIRIT; FROM EVER LASTING TO EVER LASTING. NO MAN HAS

SEEN GOD, BUT YOU SAY I LOVE HIM, AND **HATE YOUR BROTHER** WHOM YOU WALK WITH DAILY. HOW CAN THIS BE WHEN YOU DON'T EVEN LOVE HIM (GOD)? PEOPLE LOOK AT SKIN COLOR, WHO HAS THE BIGGEST BANK ACCOUNT, THE BIGGEST HOUSE, THE FINEST CAR AND EVEN THE FINEST MAN OR WOMAN; NEVER UNDERSTANDING WHAT LIFE IS ALL ABOUT. WHEN WE WAKE UP IN THE MORNING THE FIRST THING WE SHOULD DO OR SAY IS THANK YOU LORD FOR GIVING US ANOTHER DAY, INSTEAD, PEOPLE WAKE UP WITH THE SAME ATTITUDE THEY WENT TO BED WITH, DAY AFTER DAY. IF YOU ARE READING THIS, ASK GOD TO CHANGE YOUR LIFE,AND COME IN YOUR HEART, AND BE YOUR SAVIOR. **HATE** IS THE RODDEN OF A MAN BONES, IT CAN DRIVE HIM OR HER FOR THE REST OF THEIR LIVES IN TO

ALL BAD BEHAVIOR. YOU WILL NEVER LOVE YOUR FELLOW MAN UNTIL YOU FIRST LOVE YOURSELF, AND THAT IS HAVING A RELATIONSHIP WITH JESUS CHRIST, GOD'S SON. YOU FIRST HAVE TO LOVE, WITHOUT LOVE, NO MAN WILL SEE GOD. IT IS A SHAME PEOPLE OF ALL COLORS, WHO LIVE IN THIS WORLD WALK BY EACH OTHER AND DON'T EVEN NOTICE ONE ANOTHER; I MEAN IN **SPIRIT**. PEOPLE WALK BY EACH OTHER ALL DAY LONG IN THE FLESH, BUT WHEN YOU ARE IN THE SPIRIT, YOUR SMILE SHOUD SPEAK. A KIND WORD IS LOVE TO THE EARS, AND THE HEART HAS A RING OF MELODY TO IT, WHICH SWEETENS THE DAY, AND IT MAKES YOU LOVE EVERY BODY. IF WE ONLY LOVE THOSE WHO LOVE US, HOW GREAT IS THE LOVE OF GOD IN YOU? THERE IS NO GREATER LOVE THAN HE THAT IS IN YOU. THE WORLD LOVES THEIR

OWN, BUT WE THAT ARE GOD'S
CHILDREN OUGHT TO LOVE ONE
ANOTHER AND FORGIVE ONE
ANOTHER IN LOVE. I TELL YOU
PEOPLE WILL SAY I LOVE HIM OR HER,
I HAVE FORGAVE HIM OR HER; BUT
THE TRUTH OF THE MATTER IS, ONLY
GOD CAN FORGIVE. YOU WILL NEVER
BE ABLE TO LOVE OR FORGIVE,
WITHOUT THE LOVE OF GOD, AND
THAT IS "SALVATION IN JESUS." ONE
MUST KEEP HIS OR HERSELF
UNSPOTTED FROM THIS WORLD,
JESUS WANTS TO SAVE YOU, BUT
YOU FIRST HAVE TO SURRENDER
YOUR LIFE. I DON'T MEAN DIE
PHISICALLY, I MEAN SPIRITUALLY,
MANY PEOPLE COME BY WATER
ONLY, ONE MUST BE BORN-AGAIN TO
BE IN CHRIST. NOT JUST BEING TRULY
SAVED, BUT BEING BORN-AGAIN,
WHERE THE SON (JESUS CHRIST)
LIVES IN YOUR HEART. WHERE THE

HOLY GHOST (SPIRIT) IS ALIVE, SPEAKING TO OUR HEARTS,GUIDEING OUR HEARTS, AND MIND. NO LONGER BEEN ALIENATED (SEPARATED) FROM CHRIST. AT ONE TIME WE WERE NOT A PEOPLE UNTIL CHRIST DRAFTED US **("GENTILE NATION")** IN, ANY ONE CAN BE BORN-AGAIN WHO WILL ALLOW THE LOVE TO FLOW IN THEIR HEART, WITHOUT THE LOVE, THE BLOOD OF JESUS CAN'T CLEANSE YOUR SINS **("UNRIGHTEOUSNESS").** WE MUST LOVE ONE ANOTHER BEFORE WE CAN SAY WE LOVE GOD, AND BE TRUTHFUL ABOUT IT. DON'T BE LIKE THE **HYPOCRITE**, GOING AROUND PRETENDING TO BE SOMETHING WHEN HE IS NOTHING. GOD SEES ALL THAT WE DO. AND ALL THAT WE DON'T DO, IF ONE IS TO ENTER THE KINGDOM OF HEAVEN, HE MUST PURIFY HIMSELF; THAT IS TAKE UP

HIS CROSS DAILY, LOOKING FOR THAT BLESSED HOPE. I LEARN TO GIVE THE BEST OR NOTHING AT ALL, IF PEOPLE WILL LEARN THAT; THE LOVE OF CHRIST WILL FLOW IN THEIR HEART. BUT PEOPLE GIVE ONLY WHAT THEY DON'T WANT, AND MAINLY HAVE WORN OUT. PEOPLE THINK THAT THEY ARE GOING TO LOSE SO MUCH OF THEIR IDOLS, THAT IS WHAT YOUR POSSESSIONS BECOME WHEN YOU LOOK AWAY FROM GOD. LET ME EXPLAIN, IT'S NOT HARD FOR YOU TO LOVE YOUR BROTHER, SEEING HE IS IN NEED, AND YOU CAN HELP HIM OR HER; I DON'T MEAN CARRY, BUT HELP. IF WE EXAMINE OURSELVES; WE WILL SEE HOW GREATER THE LOVE IS IN US, SO LET'S BE CAREFUL TO LOVE ONE ANOTHER.

TO LOVE ONE ANOTHER IS TO LACK NOTHING

1 THESSALONIANS 4:11-12 11 And that ye study to be quiet, and to do your own business, and to work with your own hands, as we commanded you; [12] That ye may walk honestly toward them that are without, and *that* ye may have lack of nothing.

WHAT DO WE MEAN BY LACKING NOTHING, LET ME EXPLAIN IT. YOU HAVE EVERY THING THAT GOD WANTS YOU TO HAVE. YOU HAVE BEEN BLESSED WITH MONEY, A WIFE OR HUSBAND, A ROOF OVER YOUR HEAD, CLOTHES, FOOD, YOUR CHILDREN, ETC..., YOU LACK NOTHING, BECAUSE GOD HAS GIVEN YOU WHAT YOU NEED. SOME PEOPLE THINK YOU HAVE TO BE RICH IN THIS WORLD. GOD, GRACE AND MERCY IS SUFFICIENT; IT EVEN CAST OUT ALL FEAR; WHERE THE LOVE OF GOD, JESUS, AND HOLY SPIRIT CAN LIVE **(IN THE HEART OF MEN).** THIS DOESN'T COME OVER NIGHT. NOT YOU, BUT

CHRIST HAS TO TAKE YOU THROUGH
A SANTIFICATION PROCESS; WHEN
YOU GET SAVED (BORN-AGAIN) JESUS
TAKES OVER YOUR LIFE. EVEN SOME
TIMES, WE WANT TO GO OUR OWN
WAY. WE STILL HAVE A WILL, BUT
THAT WILL MUST BE IN THE CROSS
OF CHRIST, OR ELSE WE ARE
DECEIVING OURSELVES IN BELIEVING,
WE CAN DO IT ON OUR OWN. THAT'S
THE REASON SO MANY CHRISTIANS
ARE IN THE SHAPE THAT THEY ARE,
BECAUSE THEY REFUSE TO OBEY THE
GOSPEL. SOME FALL AWAY IN THE
FAITH AND SOME NEVER MAKE IT
BACK IN THE FAITH. FOLLOW JESUS,
AND YOU CAN'T GO WRONG, JESUS
WILL LEAD YOU IN THE PATH OF
RIGHTEOUSNESS. PRAY WITHOUT
CEASING, GOD KNOWS WHAT WE
NEED BEFORE WE ASK GOD FOR
WHAT WE NEED. GOD'S CHILDREN
(FOR THOSE WHO WALK IN HIS

COMMANDMENTS, AND KEEP THEM
WILL NEVER LACK NOTHING. GOD
WILL BREAK THE CURSE ON YOUR
LIFE, TEACH YOU HOW TO **LIVE** AND
GIVE. I WILL DEAL WITH THIS
SUBJECT LATER IN THE BOOK OF
(MALACHI). GOD IS ALL WE NEED, HE
(GOD) IS OUR EVERYTHING, ALL OF
GOD'S CHILDREN DOES NOT RECEIVE
ALL THAT GOD HAS FOR THEM;
BECAUSE SOME OF GOD'S CHILDREN
WILL NOT FOLLLOW GOD'S
INSTRUCTIONS. THIS IS NOT TO SAY
THAT SOME OF US ARE PERFECT BY
ANY MEANS, THIS IS SAYING SOME
ARE ON THE WRONG PATH, NOT
LISTENING TO RECEIVE WHAT GOD
HAS FOR THEM. GOD RAINS ON THE
JUST AS WELL THE UNJUST; THIS IS
NOT FAVORITISM, THIS IS GOD
DEALING WITH EACH INDIVIDUAL.
GOD GIVES HIS CHILDREN WHAT HE
(GOD) CAN TRUST THEM WITH, GOD

WILL PUT NO MORE ON US THAN
WHAT WE CAN BARE. HIS (GOD)
LOVE IS GREATER THAN OUR LOVE,
I'M GLAD HIS THOUGHTS ARE NOT
OUR THOUGHTS BECAUSE WHERE
WOULD WE BE? HE (GOD) IS
INFINITE, SEEING ALL GOOD AND
EVIL. HE IS GOD FROM EVER LASTING
TO EVER LASTING, RICH IN MERCY.
LIKE THE SONG WRITER SAY'S,
"WHEN I THINK ABOUT THE
GOODNESS OF THE LORD, WHAT HE
(GOD)HAS DONE FOR ME,
"HALLELUJAH." GOD IS SO GOOD,
NOT BECAUSE OF WHAT WE CAN GET
FROM HIM (GOD), BUT BECAUSE WE
LOVE HIM, AND THAT MAKES GOD'S
LOVE FOR US GREATER (SMILE).
BEING IN GOD'S LOVE WILL BRING
JOY, PEACE, HAPPINESS IN THE
SPIRIT, AND ALL THE GOOD THINGS
THAT GOD GIVES HIS CHILDREN.
BEING HONEST IN LIFE CARRIES A LOT

OF WEIGHT; YOU DON'T HAVE TO STEAL, LIE, CHEAT, OR COVET YOUR NEIGHBOR (PEOPLE, FRIEND, WHOMEVER). THAT'S YOUR NEIGHBOR; IF WE LACK IT IS BECAUSE THE LOVE OF GOD IS NOT IN US. NO ONE IS PERFECT, ONLY IN THE CROSS WILL WE FIND PEACE. UNDERSTANDING, IS THE BEST THING IN SEEING CLEARLY. IF WE SHARE WHAT WE HAVE WE WILL LACK NOTHING, IT'S WHEN WE TAKE OUR EYES OFF THE CROSS, IS WHEN WE BECOME GREEDY, AND GET BLIND SIDED. THERE ARE SO MANY MEN THAT ARE BLIND, WISHING THAT THEY CAN SEE. WHEN YOU ARE LIVING UNDER A CURSE, YOU ARE LIVING A MISERABLE LIFE, NOTHING SEEMS TO GO YOUR WAY. EVERYTHING IS ALWAYS GOING WRONG FOR YOU, THAT IS WHAT HAPPENS WHEN THE CHILD OF GOD

IS OUT OF GOD'S WILL. NOT TO SAY
GOD HAS FORSAKEN HIM OR HER,
BECAUSE GOD LOVES ALL HIS
CHILDREN; BUT GOD WILL CHASTISE
YOU IF YOU ARE A SON (CHILD OF
GOD). YOU BELONG TO GOD, AND
GOD WILL NOT SEE YOUR FAITH
WAVERING IN HIS LOVE; BECAUSE HE
CARES FOR YOU. HE (GOD) WILL NOT
LET YOU BE LED AWAY WITH THE
WICKED, THERE IS NO LACK IN THE
CROSS.

HYPOCRISY

WE HAVE BELIEVERS COMMITTING
FORNICATION IN THE CHURCH,
WHEN I SAY CHURCH, I MEAN SEVEN
TIMES TWENTY-FOUR. BUT PEOPLE
JUDGE SIN, THE GOOD BOOK SAYS
ALL UNRIGHTEOUSNESS IS SIN; SO IF
YOU ARE GOING TO TALK ABOUT A
PERSON'S (SIN) LET'S LOOK AT THE
WHOLE LAW OF GOD, AND NOT JUST

HOMOSEXUALITY. ALL UNRIGHTEOUSNESS IS WRONG, THE CHURCH HAS ACCEPTED SO MUCH IN GOD'S HOUSE (PEOPLE'S HEARTS).

MATTHEW 21:13 And said unto them, It is written, My house shall be called the **house of prayer;** but ye have made it a **den of thieves.**

PEOPLE HAVE GOTTEN AWAY FROM THE WORD, I MEAN THIS IS THE **LAODICEA CHURCH**, MEANING THAT IT IS NOT HOT OR COLD, BUT LUKEWARM. MANY PEOPLE BELIEVE THAT THEY ARE HEAVEN BOUND, BELEIVING IN ETERNAL SECURITY, AND LIVING ANY KIND OF WAY; GIVEN YOUR HAND TO THE PREACHER, OR JOINING A CHURCH **(ORGANIZATION)** WILL NOT GET YOU IN HEAVEN. YOU MUST BE BORN-AGAIN, KEEP ONE THING IN MIND, GOD IS NO RESPECT OF PERSON, GOD'S WORD IS NOT GOING TO TURN BACK TO HIM **"VOID"** (THAT IS

SPIT IN GOD'S FACE). HE (GOD) IS A LOVING GOD, AND ALSO A GOD OF **(WRATH)**; WHAT THE CHURCH IS TODAY IS NOT PLEASING TO GOD. TIME IS NOT STANDING STILL TO WAIT FOR NO ONE TO DECIDE TO LIVE FOR GOD. MANY MEN HAVE CHANGED THE WORD OF GOD (WATERED DOWN VERSION OF THE BIBLE). MANY MEN NO LONGER BELIEVE IN THE WORD; JUST SINGING, CALLING HIS NAME, AND PRAISING HIM WHEN YOU GET READY. YOU DON'T HAVE TO BE ON TIME, GOD SHOULD BE GLAD WHEN YOU SHOW UP. YOU GIVE GOD THE MONEY THAT YOU WANT TO GIVE, NOT BEING A CHEERFUL GIVER. SOME IN THE CHURCH CHANGE HUSBAND AND WIFE, LIKE THEY ARE CHANGING SHOES. THERE IS NO COMMITEMENT (NOT TO THE BUILDING), TO ONE ANOTHER OR

ANY WITNESSING. "YEA COME SEE US, TO OFFER YOU THE WATER DOWN VERSION OF THE BIBLE." SOME MAY SAY, "OH I'M NOT PERFECT, GOD IS NOT THROUGH WITH ME YET." YOU'VE BEEN SAYING THAT FOR THE LAST TWENTY YEARS, YOU NEED A NEW SLOGAN. OR SHE OR HE THINKS THEY ARE HOLY THAN THOU (YOU), **"YES,"** WE ARE A HOLY AND A PERICULAR PEOPLE, BE PROUD OF WHO YOU ARE IN **CHRIST**; WALK NOT IN THE WAY OF THIS WORLD, IT HAS NOTHING TO OFFER. ALL WE HAVE AND WILL EVER NEED IS IN JESUS. IT PROFITS YOU NOTHING TO GAIN THE WHOLE WORLD, YOU WILL ONLY BURN IN THE END **("TORMENTED IN THE FLAMES").** YOUR WORM CAN NEVER DIE, DON'T LET ANY ONE TELL YOU THIS IS NOT TRUE, PRAY AND ASK GOD TO REVEAL IT TO YOU IN SINCERE

PRAYER, AND GOD WILL MAKE YOU UNDERSTAND HIS WORD, ONLY IF YOU WILL BELIEVE THAT HE SENT HIS SON IN THE WORLD TO DIE FOR YOUR SINS, AND MY SINS. THERE IS NO OTHER NAME IN WHICH MAN CAN BE SAVED. THE CHURCH CAN'T GRAB YOUR HAND AND PUT YOU IN HEAVEN BY GIVING A WRITTEN CERTIFICATE, OR SIGNING YOUR NAME TO THE CHURCH LOG. YOUR NAME MUST BE **WRITTEN IN THE LAMB'S BOOK OF LIFE**. GOD WILL ONE DAY CALL THE ROLL UP YONDER, WILL YOUR NAME BE IN THE LAMB'S BOOK OF LIFE? I HOPE TO SEE YOU THERE, YOUR BROTHER IN CHRIST.

THE NATURAL MAN (CHAPTER 2)

1COR.2:14 But the natural man receiveth not the things of the Spirit of God: for they are foolishness unto him: neither can he know them, because they are spiritually discerned.

THE WORD (MAN) IN THE GR. IS WHOSOEVER: MAN, WOMAN, BOY, OR GIRL WE CAN'T LEAN ON YESTERDAY UNDERSTANDING OR EVEN YESTERDAY PITFALLS, WE MUST STRIVE FORWARD, LEAVING THOSE UNWANTED THOUGHTS THAT ONLY BRINGS US ONLY TO THE DOOR, BUT DOES NOT ALLOW GOD TO ENTER INTO ONE'S HEART, KEEPING HIM AT BAY DOES NOT STRENGTHEN OUR HEART OR MIND, BUT GIVES SATAN A FOOT HOLD IN OUR LIVES TO KEEP US

A NATURAL MAN. THE NATURAL
MAN IS BLIND, AND DECEIVED. GOD
IS NOT IMPORTANT IN HIS OR HER
LIFE, THEIR LIFE IS A ONE WAY
STREET THAT LEADS TO
DESTRUCTION, UNLESS THEY RECEIVE
GOD'S GRACE AND MERCY; THEY
WILL PERISH, THE NATURAL MAN
DOES NOT GIVE THANKS TO GOD,
PRAY, OR ASK TO RECEIVE GOD IN HIS
OR HER LIFE. WHAT MAKES A
NATURAL MAN LOOK TO HIMSELF?
ONE THING IS PRIDE AND LOW SELF-
ESTEEM THAT KEEPS A PERSON
LOOKING DOWN INSTEAD OF
LOOKING UP. HIS SELF-ESTEEM CAN
BRING HIM NOTHING BUT MISERY,
AND PAIN THAT HE OR SHE CAN'T
ENDURE, ONLY GOD CAN FILL THAT
VOID IN ONE'S LIFE. GOD CAN MAKE
THE HEART MERRY; FILL THE HEART
WITH JOY, PEACE, LOVE AND GIVE
THE NATURAL MAN FAITH THAT

ONLY IS FOUND IN THE **"CROSS."**
THAT IS WHAT KEEPS A NATURAL
MAN WHERE HE OR SHE IS AT,
BECAUSE THEY REFUSE TO LOOK TO
THE LIGHT. THEY WOULD RATHER
STAY IN DARKNESS, WHERE IT IS
ONLY GOING TO GET DARKER AND
DARKER. ONE OF THE WORST THINGS
A NATURE MAN CAN EXPERIENCE IS
SEPERATION FROM GOD, GOD GIVES
EVERY MAN A CHANCE, GOD DOES
NOT WISH THAT ANY SHOULD
PERISH, BUT TO COME TO THE CROSS
(REPENTANCE). THE NATURAL MAN'S
EARS ARE DULL OF HEARING GOD'S
CALL ON HIS OR HER LIFE, THEIR EARS
CAN ONLY HEAR WHAT THE ENEMY
HAS TO SAY BECAUSE THE NATURE
MAN IS AFRAID OF THE TRUTH, SO
THEY STAY IN DARKNESS SO THE
LIGHT WILL NOT BLIND THEM. HELL
IS A DARK PLACE, A LONELY PLACE
AND A PLACE OF TORMENT. SOME

SAY WHEN YOU'RE DEAD YOU DEAD, THIS IS NOT TRUE, THERE ARE SO MANY PEOPLE THAT ARE LOST BECAUSE THEY RECEIVED A LIE. THAT LIE HAS THEM LOCKED DOWN FOR ETERNITY IN A PLACE THAT WAS NOT MEANT FOR MAN TO GO; HELL WAS MEANT FOR SATAN, HIS ANGELS, THE DEMONS, THE FALSE PHOPHET, AND THE ANTI-CHRIST. MAN HAS PERISHED BECAUSE OF LACK OF KNOWLEDGE (FALSE KNOWLEDGE); THAT THE SPIRIT CAN'T ATTAIN. OPEN YOUR EYES, AND SEE THE LIGHT THAT SHINES OUT OF DARKNESS INTO ONE'S HEART. LET YOUR HEART BE FILLED WITH GOD'S GRACE AND MERCY, SO THAT YOUR SOUL AND SPIRIT, CAN LIVE ON FOREVER WITH THE LORD. LET HIM (JESUS) PREPARE YOU A PLACE, FOR YOU CAN'T DO ANYTHING ON YOUR OWN. EVERY THING COMES FROM

ABOVE, GOD WILL GIVE YOU THE
FREE GIFT, AND NO MAN CAN TAKE
IT AWAY FROM YOU. LET THE PEACE
FLOW IN YOUR HEART, ERASE THE
DARKNESS FROM YOUR HEART AND
LET JESUS, CAST IT IN OUTER
DARKENESS FOREVER. JUST MAKE
ONE STEP AND JESUS WILL MAKE
TWO; GIVING YOUR LIFE TO JESUS IS
THE BEST THING THAT CAN HAPPEN
TO A MAN. HE (JESUS) CAN FILL YOUR
SORROWS WITH LAUGHTER, PUT A
NEW SONG IN YOUR SOUL AND
BRING HAPPINESS IN YOUR LIFE;
THAT YOU HAVE NEVER
EXPERIENCED BEFORE. I PRAY THAT IF
YOU DON'T KNOW MY SAVIOR, JESUS
CHRIST, THAT YOU WILL COME TO
KNOW HIM (JESUS).

WHAT DOES A NATURAL MAN SEE?

"**NOTHING**" EVERY THING IS
SPIRITUALLY DISCERNED, EVERY

THING AROUND HIM OR HER IS
SPIRITUALLY DARKENED, HE OR SHE
DOES NOT LOVE (AGAPE), THE BIBLE
TELLS US IN

2TIM. 3:2 For men shall be lovers of their
own selves, covetous, boasters, proud,
blasphemers, disobedient to parents,
unthankful, unholy,

WE ARE SEEING THIS TODAY IN OUR
SOCIETY. OUR CHILDREN ARE OUT OF
CONTROL, THEIR LIFE IS ON A DOWN
HILL SPIRAL WAITING TO EXPLODE.
GOD IS KNOCKING TO COME IN THE
HEARTS OF MEN (MAN, WOMAN,
BOY, OR GIRL). THE BIBLE TELLS US
THAT IN THESE LAST DAYS WE ARE TO
WATCH AND PRAY; FOR THAT DAY
NO MAN WILL BE ABLE TO DISCERN.
MEN HEARTS WILL FAIL THEM, MEN
WILL TURN AWAY FROM GOD, AND
GO AFTER STRANGE FLESH. PEOPLE
THESE TIMES ARE HERE NOW. IT'S

NOT A POSSIBILITY THAT IT MAY
HAPPEN, IT'S HERE NOW.

**LET'S LOOK AT LOVERS OF THEIR
OWN SELVES:** LEADERS MUST NOT
BE FILLED WITH THEIR OWN
AGENDA. IT IS IMPORTANT FOR
LEADERS TO ACKNOWLEDGE GOD.
GOD MUST BE THE LEADER IN THE
HOME OF (FATHER, MOTHER, AUNT,
ETC...). ANY ONE CAN BE TEMPTED
WITH GREED OR IDOLS; THAT IS THE
REASON I SAY, A MAN HAS TO LACK
NOTHING. THAT'S WHERE THE PEACE
WILL COME. IT IS NOT IN THE IDOLS
OR THE THINGS WE POSSESS; IT IS
ALL ABOUT GOD AND HIS (GOD)
KINGDOM. WE CAN NO LONGER
SWEEP THINGS UNDER THE RUG. WE
MUST FACE THEM HEAD ON, IT'S
TIME OUT FOR PLAYING, IT'S TIME TO
GET DOWN TO BUSINESS; WE HAVE
TO BRING OUR CHILDREN BACK
HOME (CHURCH). NOT ONLY OUR

CHILDREN, BUT A LOST GENERATION. MOST PEOPLE YOUNG AND OLD IS OUT OF CONTROL. OUR YOUNG CHILDREN NEED TO SEE OUR LIVES IN TACK FIRST, THEN WE WILL BE ABLE TO TELL THEM WHAT THUS SAITH THE LORD; BUT UNTIL THEN WE ARE GOING TO CONTINUE TO GO DOWN THIS STEEP PATH. SO LET'S GET BUSY CHURCH AND LET GOD BACK IN THE HEARTS OF MEN, THANK YOU!

COVETING: IS AN EYE FULL, IT IS A DESIRE TO HAVE WHAT BELONGS TO SOMEONE ELSE. IN REALITY, IT IS WHAT WE CAN'T HAVE. COVETING CAN BE ANYTHING SUCH AS; WANTING SOMEONE'S HUSBAND, WIFE, JOB, HOME, MONEY, CAR, ETC...., JUST TO NAME A FEW, COVETING IS EVERY THING THAT DOES NOT BELONG TO YOU. MANY CHURCH (PEOPLE) STRUGGLE WITH THIS SIN. YES, PEOPLE PRACTICE THIS

24

SIN QUITE OFTEN, SOME CAN'T GET
ENOUGH. LET'S SEE WHAT COVETING
IS. FOR EXAMPLE, "THAT'S A NICE
SUIT YOU HAVE ON," ONLY WISHING
IT WAS YOUR SUIT. LET'S LOOK AT
"STEALING." THAT'S COVETING,
BECAUSE THE PERSON DID NOT GIVE
YOU PERMISSION TO TAKE, WHAT
WAS NOT GIVEN TO YOU IN THE
FIRST PLACE. THIS IS GOD'S **TENTH
AND LAST COMMANDMENT**
CHURCH.

BOASTERS: AN OPINION OF ONE'S
SELF OR BOASTING ABOUT
YOURSELF. THIS IS AN EVIL,
BRAGGART AND WICKEDNESS. WE
ARE TO LET OTHERS BRAG ON US,
AND NOT BRAG ON OURSELVES. WE
ARE TO PRAISE AND WORSHIP GOD
ONLY. GIVING ENCOURAGMENT TO
OTHERS OR RECEIVING
ENCOURAGMENT FROM OTHERS IS
FINE. BUT TO BRAG ON YOURSELF,

SOMEONE ELSE OR EVEN YOUR OWN WORKS; IS TAKING PRAISE FROM GOD AND REPLACING IT WITH YOUR OWN.

PROUD: ALWAYS FEELING ABOVE OTHERS, THIS IS PRIDE AT IT'S BEST. THIS PERSON HAS AN ARROGANT ESTEEM ABOUT HIMSELF; AND HE OR SHE NEEDS GOD IN THEIR LIFE. THEY ARE LEANING TO THEIR OWN UNDERSTANDING, GIVEN NO GROUND FOR IMPROVEMENT, AND KEEPING A PROUD LOOK. FEELING AS IF THEY ARE BETTER THAN OTHERS; WHO DON'T HAVE AS MUCH OR WHO HAVE LESS THAN THEM. WE CAN LEARN A GREAT LESSON, BY ASKING THE LORD TO TAKE THIS SIN FROM US AND FILL THIS VOID IN OUR HEARTS. THANK THE LORD FOR HE (GOD) IS GOOD AND WONDERFUL. AMEN.

BLASPHEMERS: NOT HONORING GOD, SAYING BAD THINGS ABOUT GOD. FOR EXAMPLE, SATAN SPEAKING LIES OR FALSE ACCUSATIONS AGAINST GOD. **BLASPHEMY AGAINST THE HOLY GHOST (SPIRIT)** ABOUT GOD, WAS PUNISHABLE BY DEATH, THIS SIN WAS UNPARDONABLE.

LUKE 12:10 And whosoever shall speak a word against the Son of man, it shall be forgiven him: **but unto him that blasphemeth against the Holy Ghost it shall not be forgiven.**

DISOBEDIENT TO PARENTS: MANY CHILDREN OF TODAY; HAVE NO RESPECT FOR THEMSELVES, THEIR ELDERS, OR THEIR PARENTS. WHY IS THIS? I BELIEVE, THERE HAS BEEN AN ABSENCE OF GOD AND DISCIPLINE IN THE LIVES OF MANY OF OUR CHILDREN (APOSTASY). THE LORD SAID IF WE SPARE THE ROD, WE SPOIL THE CHILD. I'M A FIRM

BELIEVER IN CORRECTING A CHILD, NOT BEATING THE CHILD; BUT FIRST SITTING AND TALKING TO THE CHILD- SO THE CHILD UNDERSTANDS WHAT SHE OR HE HAS DONE WRONG. WHEN WE DON'T DISCIPLINE OUR CHILDREN IN THE RIGHT WAY, THAT CHILD DOES NOT FEEL LOVED. DISCIPLINE DOES NOT HAVE TO BE A CORRECTION ALL THE TIME, IT DEPENDS ON THE DEGREE OF THE PUNISHMENT. LIKE I SAID, UNDERSTANDING MUST COME FIRST BEFORE DISCIPLINE. I BELIEVE THAT MAKES A CHILD BETTER. PARENTS YOU MUST START EARLY WITH THE CHILDREN AND YOU CAN'T BE THEIR FRIEND **(WORLDLY)**. BEATING A CHILD WILL NOT SEPARATE **SIN,** ONLY GOD CAN DO THAT. AS A PARENT, YOU MUST PRAY FOR YOUR CHILDREN, AND THE LORD WILL SEE THEM THROUGH. **"IT WORKS IF YOU**

DO IT GOD'S WAY." DON'T WORRY ABOUT WHAT THEY WILL DO; GOD WILL HANDLE THE SITUATION. IF YOU TEACH YOUR CHILDREN, THAT WILL TAKE A LOT OF WORRY OFF OF YOU. TRY IT AND WATCH, IT WORKS. AND ONE OTHER THING, LET YOUR CHILDREN SEE CHRIST IN YOU. PARENTING IS NOT PERFECT, YOU HAVE TO WORK AT IT. YOU WILL MAKE MISTAKES, KEEP PRAYING AND LOVING YOUR CHILD. IF YOU DON'T, THE WORLD WILL KEEP JESUS AWAY FROM YOUR CHILDREN. BY PRAYING FOR THEM, WITHOUT CEASING. REMEMBER, PARENTING STARTS WITH (DAD AND MOM). YOU HAVE TO BE PARENTS FIRST. AMEN, AMEN.

UNTHANKFUL: "YOU OWE ME" OR "I DESERVE THIS." UNGRATEFUL FOR THE THINGS THEY ALREADY HAVE. THE MORE YOU GIVE, THE MORE THEY THINK THEY DESERVE THE

THINGS, THEY HAVE NOT EARNED. WE ARE TO LOVE THE UNTHANKFUL, AS WE LOVE THOSE WHO TREAT US GOOD. THIS CAN ONLY COME FROM ABOVE, A PROCESS CALLED **"SANTIFICATION."** WHAT THE UNTHANKFUL (EVIL) DOESN'T UNDERSTAND, IS WE MUST DO THE THINGS FROM OUR HEARTS; FOR NO GAIN OF MERIT. BUT TO LOVE THE SINNER AS GOD LOVED US. IN RETURN, WE WILL BE REWARDED FOR OUR LOVE TOWARDS OUR FELLOW MAN.

UNHOLY: THE WICKED SHALL NOT INHERIT THE KINGDOM OF GOD; FOR THEIR HEART IS WICKED, IN THEM IS NO LIGHT. EVERY IMAGINATION, THEY HAVE IS WICKED. THEY CAN SEE NO GOOD, BUT EVIL CONTINUOUSLY. WHEN THEY GET UP IN THE MORNING, TO THE GOING DOWN OF THE SUN (BED TIME); THEIR HEART IS

CONTINUOUSLY EVIL IN THE SIGHT OF GOD. THE REJECTION OF THE CROSS, HAS NO MERIT (GRACE) WITH THEM. THEY WON'T OPEN THEIR EYES TO SEE THE GOODNESSS OF THE LORD OR HEAR THE WORDS OF THE LORD; THAT THEY MIGHT BE SAVED. **"I TELL YOU,"** DON'T LET THE SUN GO DOWN UPON YOUR WRATH, FOR THE LORD SHALL DESTROY THE WICKED WHEN HE RETURNS THE SECOND TIME.

HOW TO PUT ON THE WHOLE ARMOUR OF GOD (CHAPTER 3)

LET ME TELL YOU WHAT THUS SAITH THE LORD.

MATT.4:4 BUT HE ANSWERED AND SAID, IT IS WRITTEN, MAN (WOMAN, BOY, OR GIRL) SHALL NOT LIVE BY **BREAD ALONE, BUT BY EVERY WORD THAT PROCEEDETH OUT OF THE MOUTH OF GOD**.

THIS IS THE FULL ARMOR OF GOD, I DID NOT KNOW THIS UNTIL THE LORD OPENED MY EYES TO SEE THE TRUTH ABOUT HIS (GOD) WORD. GOD TOLD ME THAT I WAS LIVING BY BREAD ALONE; I THOUGHT HE MEANT BREAD, NO HE MEANT **"DEATH."** THERE ARE MILLIONS AND MILLIONS, THAT ARE IN THIS BOAT; CAUGHT UP WITHOUT A PADDLE. I

FINALLY RECEIVED WHAT GOD HAD
FOR ME, AND THAT IS THE TRUTH
ABOUT HIS WORD. YOU SEE I WAS
NO LONGER LEANING TO MY OWN
UNDERSTANDING. THIS DIDN'T
HAPPEN OVER NIGHT, I HAD TO FIRST
REALIZE AND BELIEVE GOD'S WORD;
SO I COULD BE SET FREE FROM THE
LIES OF THIS WORLD. I CONTINUED
DAILY, SEEKING THE TRUTH. PRAYING
IN THE SPIRIT AND WAITING
PATIENTLY FOR THE WORD TO COME
TO ME; TO GUIDE ME IN ALL TRUTH.
THIS SET ME FREE. **"YES,"** I WAS
SAVED BUT I WAS RETURNING TO MY
OWN **"VOMMIT."** LIKE MANY
CHRISTIANS, THEY BELIEVE THEY ARE
SAVED; BUT DO NOT HAVE THE
WHOLE ARMOUR OF GOD ON. TO
MAKE IT PLAIN AND SIMPLE, THE
TRUTH IS THE FURTHEST THING
FROM OUR MINDS. SATAN HAS HID
THE GOSPEL FROM YOU, THAT YOUR

MIND HAS BECOME BLINDED TO THE THINGS OF GOD, THE BIBLE TELLS US IN

2COR.4:3-4 But if our gospel be hid, it is hid to them that are lost: [4] In whom the god of this world hath blinded the minds of them which believe not, lest the light of the glorious gospel of Christ, who is the image of God, should shine unto them.

MANY PEOPLE CONFESS GOD WITH THEIR MOUTH, BUT THEIR HEARTS ARE DARK AND FULL OF SIN; THAT ONLY JESUS CHRIST, CAN TAKE AWAY. GOD WANTS TO BE IN CONTROL OF YOUR LIFE. YOU CAN'T JUST GO TO CHURCH ON SUNDAY, THIS IS A FULL TIME JOURNEY. SATAN DOES NOT STOP, WHILE YOU ARE RESTING. HE IS CONSTANLY DECEIVING AND THAT'S THE REASON WE NEED TO PRAY WITHOUT

CEASING; BECAUSE THE ENEMY
WANTS TO STEALL OUR SOUL. THE
BIBLE TELLS US; THAT HE (SATAN)
COMES TO STEAL, KILL, AND
DESTROY. I (JESUS) COME THAT YOU
MIGHT HAVE LIFE MORE
ABUNDANTLY. THE BIBLE TELLS US
THAT WE ARE TO WATCH AND PRAY
ALWAYS; LOOKING FOR THAT
BLESSED HOPE THAT IS IN US, FOR
THOSE THAT LOVE HIS COMING. ONE
DAY JESUS IS COMING BACK FOR HIS
CHURCH, WITHOUT SPOT OR
WRINKLE. HOW MANY WILL BE
READY? I DON'T USE THE WORD
TRULY, BECAUSE YOU ARE EITHER
SAVED OR UNSAVED; THERE IS NO
NEUTRAL GROUND. THAT IS THE
BIGGEST LIE TOLD TODAY, THAT
KEEPS MAN SEPERATED FROM GOD'S
LOVE. IF WE WOULD LOOK TO THE
BIBLE AND BELIEVE EVERY WORD
THAT PROCEEDETH OUT THE MOUTH

OF GOD, WE WILL BE SAVED FROM THIS EVIL AND DARK WORLD, THAT SATAN HAS MADE EVIL. GOD WANTS TO SHINE HIS LIGHT IN YOUR HEART, **"THAT LIVING WATER."** SEE THE FATHER (GOD), HAS GIVEN JESUS THE POWER, THAT HE (JESUS) SHOULD LOOSE NOTHING. WE SHOULD HAVE OUR TRUST TOTALLY IN JESUS, FOR HE IS THE AUTHOR OF OUR FAITH. (FINISHER) OF ALL THAT WE HAVE IN CHRIST, FOR THE CROSS HAS MADE IT POSSIBLE FOR US TO LIVE AND BE SAVED FROM THIS DARK AND EVIL WORLD. ONLY GOD CAN SEE YOU THROUGH, SO OBEY HIS WORD AND LIVE FOREVER IN ETERNITY.

WHAT DOES THE WORD ABUNDANTLY MEAN?:

"HAVING PLENTY", AND MORE THAN ENOUGH OF JESUS. I AM THE DOOR THAT LEADS TO LIFE. DEATH HAS NO

PLACE BUT THE LAKE OF FIRE. LOOK
AROUND AND SIT DOWN. OPEN
YOUR EYES AND EARS. TAKE A DEEP
BREATH, (GOD IS ALL AROUND US);
BUT SATAN WANTS TO KEEP YOU IN
BONDAGE. HE (SATAN) IS TRYING TO
WIN YOUR "SOUL." IF ANY
MAN,WOMAN, BOY OR GIRL ENTERS
IN AT THE DOOR; THEY SHALL BE
SAVED. THE BIBLE TELLS US THAT THE
NATURE MAN WALKS IN HIS OWN
SELFISH WAYS; ASKING NO ONE AND
NO BODY FOR HELP. HE'S
CONSTANTLY PLAYING ON OTHERS,
LIKE THE GAMES PEOPLE PLAY IN
LIFE. HE WATCHES OUT FOR NO ONE
BUT HIMSELF. HE GIVES NOTHING,
BUT ONLY TAKES FROM OTHERS. HE
LOOKS ONLY TO THE DAY, WHEN HE
CAN COUNT ONLY ON HIMSELF;
WHEN HE THINKS THIS LIFE IS OVER.
THERE IS NO NEUTRAL GROUND.
THERE IS LIFE AFTER DEATH. SATAN

HAS HIM OR HER LOOKING DOWN A
LONESOME ROAD, FILLED WITH
NOTHING BUT LIES. THE NATURAL
MAN IS TORMENTED (MIND) ON A
DAILY BASIS; NEVER COMING TO THE
TRUTH. MAN'S HEART IS DARK, HE
HATES THE LIGHT, THAT CAN BRING
HIM TO A SAVING GRACE. BEING ONE
("NOT BEING DOUBLE-MINDED")
WITH THE FATHER, SON, AND HOLY
SPIRIT. LIFTING HIM OR HER OUT OF
DARKNESS AND THE BONDAGE, THAT
KEEPS THEM FROM RECEIVING
GOD'S PLAN OF SALVATION. THAT
WONDERFUL AND GLORIOUS SPIRIT,
THAT SETS ALL MEN FREE. ALL YOU
HAVE TO DO IS ASK FOR IT. IT IS
GIVEN TO ALL THAT WILL RECEIVE
THE GIFT OF ETERNAL LIFE, **WITH THE
TRINITY**. ASK HIM TO TAKE YOUR
HAND AND THE LORD WILL PLACE
YOUR HAND IN HIS HANDS. AND WILL
GIVE YOU ALL THE THINGS IN THIS

LIFE THAT IT HAS TO OFFER. THE
LORD'S HAND, IS BIGGER THAN OUR
HANDS. THE LORD CAN FILL ALL
YOUR NEEDS AND GIVE YOU JOY
THAT YOU NEVER HAD BEFORE. THE
LORD GIVES ALL HIS CHILDREN
PEACE. THIS IS A FEELING THAT GETS
ALL OVER YOUR BODY; PEOPLE CAN
SEE THIS, BUT A LOT OF PEOPLE
CAN'T UNDERSTAND IT. GET TO
KNOW THE LORD, HE (LORD) WANTS
TO LOVE (AGAPE) YOU AND KEEP
YOU FOREVER AND FOREVER. THE
ENEMY CAN'T TOUCH ANYTHING
THAT BELONGS TO GOD. GOD HAS
THE FIRST, LAST AND FINAL SAY SO;
OVER WHAT HAPPENS, TO WHAT
BELONGS TO HIM (GOD). NOTHING IS
TOO HARD FOR GOD, NOTHING CAN
STAND IN THE WAY OF GOD. THE
(LORD) IS ALL KNOWING, ALL
POWERFUL AND ALL PRESENCE. THE
(LORD) IS EVERYWHERE, AND THE

(LORD) WILL BE WITH YOU TO THE END. THE (LORD) WILL NOT FORSAKE YOU OR LEAVE YOU. THE LORD IS A FRIEND TO THE END; THE LORD WILL COMFORT YOU IN ALL OF YOUR TROUBLES. THE LORD WILL KEEP YOU AND BUILD A PROTECTION AROUND YOU. IN THIS WORLD, ALL YOU NEED IS FAITH. YOU TRIED YOUR WAY AND YOU FAILED TIME AFTER TIME. GIVE GOD A CHANCE TO MAKE IT RIGHT, YOU WILL NEVER BE ABLE TO OVER COME THE ENEMY ON YOUR OWN. SATAN WILL FOREVER DECEIVE YOU IN BELIEVING, THINGS ARE BETTER ON THE OTHER SIDE. SO MANY PEOPLE THAT ARE SUCCESFUL, HAVE BOUGHT INTO THIS LIFE **(LIE).** HE WILL PROMISE YOU THE WORLD, WHICH HE DOES NOT OWN. SATAN'S WORLD IS ONLY THE LAKE OF FIRE **(DEATH)**. OUR WARFARE IS NOT CARNAL, BUT SPIRITUAL. YOU CAN'T

FIGHT THE ENEMY WITH A WEAPON OR A BUNKER. SATAN IS A SPIRIT, AND HE HAS BEEN GIVEN POWER IN THIS WORLD FOR A SHORT TIME. THE ONLY WAY YOU ARE GOING TO DEFEAT THE ENEMY, IS THROUGH THE CROSS **(JESUS CHRIST).** THERE IS NO OTHER WAY OR NAME UNDER THE SUN, THAT MAN CAN BE SAVED, EXCEPT BY THE **"BLOOD"** (JESUS CHRIST). THE BLOOD IS WHAT CLEANSED US, AND MADE US WHOLE IN THE EYES OF GOD. WITHOUT THE BLOOD, YOU CAN'T SEE GOD. NO UNCLEAN THING CAN AND WILL NOT ENTER IN THE KINGDOM OF HEAVEN. RELIGION WON'T GET YOU THERE; YOUR CHURCH WON'T GET YOU THERE. YOUR FRIENDS, YOUR FAMILY NOR YOUR MONEY WON'T GET YOU THERE. THE PREACHER CAN'T GET YOU IN. MANY PREACH EVERY SUNDAY THAT YOU ARE ALL RIGHT;

BUT THE WAGES OF **SIN IS DEATH**.
DON'T LET SATAN'S LIES KEEP YOU
OUT OF THAT CITY CALLED **THE HOLY
CITY NEW JERUSALEM**. THIS IS
DIFFERENT FROM THE JERUSALEM
ON THE EARTH TODAY. FOR ALL OF
THE EARTH WILL BE BURNED UP.
GOD WILL BUILD (SPEAK IN TO
EXISTENCE) THE CITY THAT WE WILL
LIVE IN FOR ETERNITY; FOR THOSE
WHO HAVE BEEN WASHED WITH THE
BLOOD,THE LAMB OF JESUS CHRIST.
IF I WAS YOU, I WOULD MAKE THIS
CHOICE TODAY; TO PUT ON THE
WHOLE ARMOUR OF GOD, **"AND
THAT IS EVERY WORD THAT
PROCEEDETH OUT OF THE MOUTH
OF GOD."** MANY MEN HAVE WAITED.
I'LL DO IT TOMORROW, THE NEXT
DAY, OR THE NEXT. GOD'S TIME
CLOCK IS NOT OUR TIME, WE DON'T
HAVE A SECOND TO LOSE. SATAN IS A
ROARING LION, SEEKING WHO HE

(SATAN) MAY DEVOUR. SATAN HAS
DECEIVED SO MANY PEOPLE AND
CUNNED SO MANY PEOPLE OUT OF
THEIR SALVATION. QUIT LOOKING
BACK AND LOOK FORWARD TO THAT
BLESSED HOPE, OF OUR LORD AND
SAVIOR JESUS CHRIST; WHO TAKES
AWAY ALL THE SINS OF THE WORLD.
WHO (JESUS) GIVES TO MEN FREELY,
THE GIFT OF ETERNITY.

**PUT ON THE ARMOUR (WHOLE) OF
GOD**

WE MUST **FIRST** TAKE THE WHOLE
ARMOUR OF GOD, BY EVERY WORD
OF GOD'S **(MOUTH).** WITH OUT THIS
YOU WILL BE FIGHTING CARNALLY, IN
STEAD OF SPIRITUALLY. WE ARE NOT
DEALING WITH BLOOD, THESE
DEMONS ARE REAL; SO PRAY UP
BEFORE ENTERING THIS FIGHT OR
YOU WILL BE DEFEATED, BEFORE YOU
LEAVE THE GATE. REMEMBER **GOD**

HAS TO BE FIRST. "GIVE GOD PRAISE" FOR WHAT HE (GOD) IS ABOUT TO DO IN YOUR LIFE.

IN EPHESIANS, THE SIX CHAPTER, VERSES TEN THROUGH SEVENTEEN; GOD TELLS US SIX THINGS TO PREPARE FOR BATTLE.

A. **OUR LOINS SHOULD BE OF TRUTH**
   THERE SHOULD BE NO GOSSIP IN OUR LIFE. GOSSIP IS NOT OF THE TRUTH, IT SPREADS LIES TO EVERY CORNER IN ONE'S LIFE. THE TONGUE MUST BE TAMED BEFORE WE ARE ABLE TO SPREAD THE GOSPEL; OR ELSE YOU WILL FIND YOUR SELF WORKING FOR SATAN, INSTEAD OF GOD. EVERY SEED MUST BE ON GOOD GROUND, IN ORDER FOR THE WORD OF GOD TO TAKE EFFECT IN ONE'S LIFE. GOSSIP HURTS PEOPLE BECAUSE IT SPREADS LIES, THAT

PEOPLE DO NOT HAVE FACTS TO BACK UP; THE WORDS THAT HURT OTHER PEOPLE. REMEMBER, THE HEART IS EVIL; WE MUST BE CARFUL WITH GOD'S WORD IN OUR LIFE, AS WELL AS OTHERS.

B. **OUR BREASTPLATE SHOULD BE FILLED WITH RIGHTEOUSNESS** THAT WE LIE NOT TO ONE ANOTHER, AND THE FLESH MUST BE CRUCIFIED BEFORE WE CAN DO THE WORK THAT IS FILLED IN OUR HEART FOR CHRIST. CHRIST MUST BE THE CAPTAIN OF THE SHIP, OR YOU RISK SHIP WRECK. WE ARE CRUCIFIED TO THE WORLD; WE LIVE IN THIS WORLD, BUT NOT OF THIS WORLD. DO NOT ATTEMPT TO WORK FOR CHRIST IN THE FLESH, IT WILL ONLY BRING **DEATH** TO THOSE WHO ARE FOLLOWING YOU. LEAN NOT TO YOUR OWN UNDERSTANDING, IT

WILL ONLY BRING OUT YOUR
OWN BELIEF IN A BAD WAY; THAT
DOES NOT BRING THE SINNER TO
CHRIST. WITHOUT
RIGHTEOUSNESS, IT WILL LEAD
YOU TO ALL KINDS OF LUST.

C. **YOUR FEET WITH THE GOSPEL OF PEACE**

WE ARE THE CHILDREN OF GOD,
BECAUSE WE SPREAD PEACE
AMONG THE BRETHREN. NO
PERSON IS A PEACE MAKER; WHO
DIVIDES A COUNTRY, FAMILY,
MARRIAGE, CHURCH, CHILDREN,
ETC... WE MUST COMFORT AND
LOVE ONE ANOTHER BEFORE WE
WILL BE ABLE TO SEE GOD.
WITHOUT LOVE IT IS IMPOSSIBLE.
THE WORLD IS GROWING COLDER
EVERY DAY. THE LAODICEA
CHURCH IS NOT HOT OR COLD, SO
HOW CAN IT BRING PEACE TO A
DYING WORLD, WHEN THE

CHURCH ITSELF IS DEAD?

REVELATION 3:20 Behold, I stand at the door, and knock: if any man hear my voice, and open the door, I will come in to him, and will sup with him, and he with me.

BEHOLD, I (GOD) STAND AT THE DOOR, AND KNOCK, THIS VERSE IS IN REALITY TALKING TO **BELIEVERS;** TO LET GOD BACK INTO THEIR LIVES. THEY HAVE GONE ASTRAY, AND GOD IS **SAYING** OPEN THE DOOR; SO I-THE LORD, CAN COME IN AND LOVE YOU. ONLY GOD, CAN BRING PEACE IN ONE'S LIFE.

D. **THE SHIELD OF FAITH**

THE SHIELD GUARDS AND PROTECTS OUR BODY, FROM THE FIERY DARTS. THE WICKED WATCHES THE RIGHTEOUS EVERY MOVEMENT, WHEN THE WICKED IS IN POWER. THE RIGHTEOUS HAS TO KEEP THEIR SHIELD UP READY FOR COMBAT WITH THE

ADVERSARY. WE MUST LOVE OUR
ENEMIES, AND HATE THE SIN. OUR
FAITH MUST BE WITHOUT FEAR
OF THE WICKED; KEEPING OUR
MIND AND HEART ON GOD. FOR
HE (GOD) IS A SHIELD TO THEM
WHO TRUST HIM DAILY; TO
RENEW THEIR STRENGTH. HIS
STRENGTH IS OUR SHIELD.

E. **THE HELMET OF SALVATION**
   JESUS IS THE ROCK OF OUR
   SALVATION. TO EVERYONE WHO
   PUTS THEIR TRUST IN HIM (JESUS).
   THE HELMET GUARDS US FROM
   ALL CONDEMNATION, THAT THE
   FLESH BRINGS DAILY IN OUR
   LIVES. IT GUARDS OUR MIND AND
   CORRECTS OUR THOUGHTS. IT
   BRINGS JOY TO OUR HEART AND
   MIND. IT FREES US FROM THE
   LAW AND DEATH. SIN NO LONGER
   RULES OUR LIFE. WE ARE SET FREE
   BY THE BLOOD (JESUS CHRIST).

FOR WE NO LONGER WALK IN THE FLESH, BUT AFTER THE SPIRIT.

F. THE SWORD OF THE SPIRIT (THE WORD OF GOD)

OUR WEAPONS ARE NOT CARNAL, BUT ARE SPIRITUAL; FOR GOD FIGHTS OUR BATTLES. OUR ENEMIES DON'T UNDERSTAND HOW WE KEEP GETTING UP, BLOW AFTER BLOW. JESUS SHIELDS US FROM ALL HARM AND DANGER. DAVID FOUGHT THE PHILLISTINE; HE HAD A SPEAR, SWORD AND SHIELD. BUT DAVID CAME IN THE NAME OF THE LORD OF HOSTS, FOR OUR BATTLE IS NOT OURS, BUT THE LORD'S. DAVID TOOK HIS ARMOUR OFF, STOOD ON THE PROMISES OF GOD, AND WAS VICTORIOUS. GOD WILL FIGHT YOUR BATTLE IF YOU JUST BE STILL.

SALVATION ONLY IN JESUS (CHAPTER 4)

WHAT IS SALVATION: SALVATION IS ETERNAL LIFE ONLY BY JESUS CHRIST.

ROMANS 6:23 For the wages of sin *is* **death;** but the gift of God *is* **eternal life through Jesus Christ our Lord.**

IT ONLY COMES BY GOD'S GRACE, THERE IS NOTHING WE CAN DO TO EARN OUR SALVATION. MEN LOOK TO THEMSELVES, EVEN DECEIVE THEMSELVES; BUT GOD KNOWS THE HEART AND SOUL OF MAN. GOD HAS THE FIRST AND LAST WORD. THE BIBLE TELLS US, DON'T BELIEVE THE LIE THAT SATAN HAS PLACED IN YOUR MIND. ONCE YOU START BELIEVING THE LIE, IT ENTERS YOUR HEART, AND YOU BECOME CALLOUS (HARDENED). WE MUST NOT LEAN

TO OUR ON UNDERSTANDING; IT ONLY LEADS TO SIN, AND MORE SIN. WHAT DOES SIN DO IN OUR LIVES? IT BRINGS ON DEATH. THERE IS TOO MANY PEOPLE THAT ARE NOT SAVED BECAUSE THEY WON'T TRUST IN GOD; TO DO THE WORK IN THEIR LIVES. THIS IS CALLED **"SANTIFICATION."** TRUSTING GOD IS THE ONLY WAY FOR MAN TO BECOME ONE **("NOT BEING DOUBLE-MINDED")** WITH GOD. WITHOUT THE SPIRIT OF GOD IN ONE'S LIFE, HE OR SHE CAN NOT BE SAVED. THEY HAVE NO PART WITH JESUS CHRIST. THE REAL PROBLEM WITH MAN IS THAT HE WANTS TO GUIDE HIMSELF. MANY CHURCHES TODAY HAS BECOME ABOUT "FASHION." WHAT I MEAN IS, **("WORLDLY").** MANY CHURCHES HAVE ALLOWED EVERY THING TO COME IN THE CHURCH, EXCEPT GOD. AND HAVE PUSHED

GOD SO FAR OUT THE CHURCH, THAT HE STAND AT THE DOOR AND KNOCKS. WHY IS THE WORLD BEING ALLOWED IN THE CHURCH;WHILE GOD STANDS AT THE DOOR, ON THE OUTSIDE? THE CHURCH IS NOT JUST SUNDAY MORNING, WENESDAY NIGHT OR ANY OTHER DAY OF THE WEEK. CHURCH IS TWENTY-FOUR HOURS A DAY, SEVEN DAYS A WEEK. IT IS A RELATIONSHIP WITH THE SAVIOR JESUS CHRIST, BECAUSE HE LIVES IN OUR HEARTS AND NOT JUST OUR MINDS. WE ARE TO GIVE AN ACOUNT FOR OUR SIN AND NOT JUSTIFY THEM; ONLY DECEIVING OURSELVES. FOR THE WORD OF GOD IS TO BE PURE IN OUR HEARTS, SO THERE IS NO **SPIRITUAL ADULTERY:** MEANING WHEN **BELIEVERS** TURN THEIR LOVE FROM GOD TO SOMEONE OR SOMETHING ELSE. THAT IS THE REASON WE MUST KEEP

OUR EYES ON THE CROSS; FOR OUR
SALVATION IS THROUGH THE
"BLOOD." THERE IS NO OTHER NAME
GIVEN, WHERE WE CAN RECEIVE
SALVATION. JESUS IS OUR REFUGE,
BUNKER, SHIELD, STRONGHOLD,
EVERYTHING, ETC. IF WE ARE
WITHOUT CHASTISEMENT, THEN ARE
YE BASTARDS AND NOT SONS. EVIL
HAS YOUR LIFE ALL TANGLED, THAT
YOU CAN'T MAKE A RIGHT DECISION.
EVERY TIME THE LIGHT COMES ON,
SPIRITUAL DARKNESS PULLS YOU
FURTHER AWAY FROM THE TRUTH.
THE BIBLE TELLS US TO PUT ON THE
WHOLE ARMOUR OF GOD. MANY
CHRISTIANS, BELIEVERS, CHURCH
GOERS ETC.... BELIEVE THEY HAVE
THE WHOLE ARMOUR OF GOD ON.
FIRST, WHAT IS THE WHOLE ARMOUR
OF GOD? THE REASON I ASK THIS
QUESTION IS: I SEE SO MANY
CHRISTIANS (BELIEVERS) IN

BONDAGE (DARKNESS). THEY DON'T
KNOW HOW TO LIVE FOR GOD, OR
PUT ON THE WHOLE ARMOUR OF
GOD. I KNOW YOU HAVE BEEN
TAUGHT IN YOUR CHURCH, BIBLE
STUDY, SUNDAY SCHOOL, ETC. BUT
THERE IS A RIGHT WAY TO HONOR
GOD'S WORD. MANY PEOPLE ARE
NOT BEING TAUGHT THE WORD OF
GOD; THEY ARE ONLY GETTING A
WATERED DOWN VERSION OF THE
WORD OF GOD. THERE ARE TO MANY
SPIRITS THAT PEOPLE HAVE. WHAT I
MEAN IS, THERE ARE DIVISIONS
AMONG US IN THE CHURCH THAT
SHOULD NOT BE THERE. WE SHOULD
BE OF ONE SPIRIT IN CHRIST.
"LISTEN," THERE IS GOING TO BE NO
WAY THAT ALL THE CHRISTIANS WILL
ENTER IN THE KINGDOM OF HEAVEN,
WITH ALL KIND OF SPIRITS;
CONFESSING TO KNOW JESUS
CHRIST. YOU MUST HAVE THE SPIRIT

OF CHRIST TO BE SAVED **("BORN-AGAIN")** OR YOU HAVE NO PART WITH THE FATHER, SON, AND HOLY SPIRIT. I HOPE SOMEONE IS LISTENING TO GOD'S WORD, AND NOT BELIEVING WHAT PEOPLE OR FALSE PREACHERS ARE SAYING. EVERY ONE HAS THEIR OWN GOD, BUT THERE IS ONLY ONE GOD. I HAVE STUDIED ENOUGH TO KNOW THIS TO BE TRUE. I BEG YOU TO ASK FOR WISDOM FROM THE LORD, AND MAKE HIM THE LORD OF YOUR LIFE. DON'T SETTLE FOR, "THAT'S THE WAY IT IS." **"NO,"** THAT'S NOT THE WAY IT IS. JESUS IS COMING BACK FOR HIS CHURCH ONE DAY, AND ONLY THE **"PURE IN HEART"** WILL BE CAUGHT UP TO MEET JESUS IN THE AIR. IF YOU DIE BEFORE THE RAPTURE, "**WATCH**" MEANS TO BE READY; TO PURIFY YOURSELF FROM THIS EVIL WORLD THAT HAS NO LOVE FOR JESUS. WE

MUST CLEANSE OUR SELVES FROM
ALL UNRIGHTEOUSNESS. WE MUST
WALK DAILY WITH JESUS. THE
PROBLEM IS, WE CAN'T TELL THE
WORLD FROM THE CHURCH TODAY.
MANY PEOPLE DON'T WANT TO CALL
SIN BY IT'S NAME. THIS IS ONLY A
FORM OF GODINESS, ONLY THE
TRUTH WILL MAKE YOU FREE. I PRAY
THAT YOU WILL FIND JESUS CHRIST
AND MAKE JESUS THE LORD OF YOUR
LIFE. GIVE THIS EVIL AND DARK
WORLD UP; REPENT AND TURN BACK
TO GOD. FOR HE CARES FOR YOU
AND GOD WILL WASH ALL THE SINS
AWAY, AND WILL NOT REMEMBER
YOUR SINS ANYMORE. IF YOU DO
NOT REPENT, YOU WILL HAVE NO
PART WITH HIM **("GOD THE FATHER,
GOD THE SON, AND GOD THE HOLY
SPIRIT."** PEOPLE THINK THEY CAN
KEEP ON DOING THE THINGS
BECAUSE I'M SAVED. **"NO, GOD**

FORBID," MEANING THAT WE CAN'T KEEP ON LIVING APART FROM HIM, AND LIVE WITH GOD FOR EVER AND EVER. THE BIBLE DOES NOT TEACH THAT A MAN CAN BUILD HIS ON KINGDOM. GOD'S WORD IS PLAIN IN SCRIPTURE, AND IT TELLS US THAT THE WAGES OF SIN IS **"DEATH."** WITHOUT GOD'S SON, THERE IS NO SALVATION. YOU CAN TAKE A BATH IN ALL THE WATER YOU WANT, GIVE THE PREACHER YOUR HAND AND HAVE YOUR NAME ON MAN'S ROLL OF **"HIS CHURCH,"** YOU WILL NEVER ENTER INTO THE KINGDOM OF HEAVEN. THE WORD OF GOD IS BASED ON **"ACCORDING TO MY GOSPEL."** THERE ARE SO MANY PEOPLE WAKING UP FROM DEATH, TO FIND OUT THEY HAVE BEEN DECEIVED. "I'M A GOOD PERSON", "WE ALL HAVE SIN" OR "NO ONE IS PERFECT." YES, ALL OF THIS IS TRUE;

THAT'S THE REASON THERE IS A
"SANTIFICATION PROCESS." WE
MUST BE PURIFIED, AND ONLY JESUS
CAN FIX OUR LIFE. IF YOU HAVE THAT
ATTITUDE, THEN YOU SHOULD HAVE
STAYED IN THE WORLD. NO ONE IS
FIT FOR THE KINGDOM, WHO
RETURNS BACK TO HIS OLD WAYS.
THAT'S THE REASON GOD SAID IN HIS
WORD, THAT WE ARE A NEW
CREATURE. "**REPENT,**" SO GOD CAN
USE YOU FOR HIS KINGDOM AND
QUIT LISTENING TO THE WORLD. THE
WORLD IS EVEN IN MANY CHURCHES.
SATAN HAS DECEIVED AND
DISGUISED THE WORD OF GOD, SO
THAT A "**CARNAL MAN**" (BELIEVER)
CAN'T TELL THE DIFFERENCE.
BECAUSE HE HAS NOT THE SPIRIT OF
CHRIST, ONLY A FORM OF
GODLINESS. YOU CAN BE WHAT EVER
YOU WANT TO BE; MASKING UP ON
SUNDAY FOR CHURCH, BIBLE STUDY

OR SUNDAY SCHOOL WILL NOT MAKE YOU A CHRISTIAN. YOU MUST BE "**BORN-AGAIN**" (THE FLESH BEING CRUCIFIED). PEOPLE ARE LOST TODAY BECAUSE THEY WILL NOT LISTEN TO SOUND DOCTRINE. MANY PEOPLE ARE NOW GETTING THEIR IMFORMATION FROM THE INTERNET. I'M NOT SAYING THE INTERNET IS BAD OR WRONG; WHAT I'M SAYING IS THAT YOU SHOULD SEEK SOUND DOCTRINE. BE CAREFUL OF THE THINGS YOU HEAR AND SEE. AND MOST OF ALL, THE PEOPLE THAT YOU ALLOW IN YOUR CIRCLE. THE BIBLE TELLS US, NOT TO BE UNEQUALLY YOKED WITH UNBELIEVERS. SOME WILL SAY, "WHAT'S WRONG WITH THAT?" THEY MAY BE A GOOD PERSON OR BELIEVE IN KINDNESS. ALL OF THAT IS GOOD, "**EXCEPT**" THEY WILL DRIVE YOU AWAY FROM GOD, WITH THEIR UNGODLY WAYS.

THIS HAPPENED TO SOLMON IN THE
BIBLE, THE WOMEN HAD THEIR OWN
"**GOD.**" THIS IS WHAT GOD IS
SAYING, I HAVE LEARNED THAT
GOD'S WORD IS TRUE AND FAITHFUL.
THERE IS NO FAILURE IN GOD'S
WORD. YOU CAN COUNT IT UP AND
TAKE IT TO THE BANK; THE FAILURE IS
IN MAN. GOD WON'T AND WILL NOT
TOLERATE ANY SIN, ENTERING THE
KINGDOM OF HEAVEN. LISTEN TO
GOD'S WORD. GOD'S WORD IS THE
ONLY TRUTH THAT CAN SAVE MAN.
NO ONE CAN SAVE YOU BUT GOD. A
PREACHER CAN NOT SAVE YOU. HE
CAN LEAD YOU TO GOD'S WORD BUT
HE CAN'T MAKE YOU ACCEPT GOD IN
YOUR HEART. YOU CAN PUT ALL THE
MONEY IN CHURCH, PAY TITHES AND
GIVE ALL THAT YOU HAVE; THE ONLY
THING THAT WILL GET YOU IN THE
KINGDOM, IS YOUR FAITH IN THE
WORD OF GOD. AND THAT IS THE

SON OF GOD, OUR LORD AND
SAVIOR, JESUS CHRIST. LET'S LOOK AT
LYING FOR INSTANCE; LYING IS A
SPIRIT, LIKE ALL THE REST OF THE
SINS. NO SIN IS GREATER OR
SMALLER THAN THE OTHER. GOD
CALLS IT ALL UNRIGHTOUSNESS;
THEY ARE ALL ABOMINATIONS UNTO
HIM. I HAVE HEARD SOME PEOPLE
SAY THAT THERE ARE DEGREES IN
HELL, THIS IS TRUE, THE BIBLE
TEACHES THIS. SEPERATION FROM
GOD FOR ETERNITY IS BAD ENOUGH,
AND I COULDN'T IMAGINE BEING
SEPERATED FROM GOD, LIVING
WITHOUT MY SAVIOR JESUS CHRIST,
AND BEING WITHOUT THE HOLY
SPIRIT. SOME PEOPLE SAY WHEN
YOU'RE DEAD, YOU'RE DEAD. MY
SPIRIT AND SOUL TELLS ME THAT
THERE IS A GOD, BECAUSE JESUS
LIVES IN SIDE OF ME. JESUS WALKS
WITH ME AND HE TALKS TO MY

SPIRIT. JESUS SAVED MY SOUL AND
DID FOR ME, WHAT I COULDN'T DO
FOR MYSELF. GAVE ME A NEW
NAME, A NEW WALK AND A NEW
TALK. I AM NO LONGER THE SAME,
JESUS CHANGED MY WHOLE LIFE.
AND NOW I'M FREE TO SERVE JESUS,
THE SON OF THE LIVING GOD. A
SALVATION CHECK: ARE YOU
SERVING MORE THAN ONE GOD, AND
NOT THE ONLY GOD OF THIS
UNIVERSE? THEN YOU NEED A
SALVATION CHECK, **"OH YES,"** JESUS
IS REAL. DO THIS FOR ME, ASK HIM
TO COME IN YOUR HEART AND MEAN
IT WITH ALL YOUR MIGHT AND SOUL.
AND SEE THE RESULTS. I DARE YOU
TO TRY HIM **"(JESUS)."** YOUR LIFE
WILL NEVER BE THE SAME; YOU WILL
HAVE JOY AND PEACE THAT YOU
HAVE NEVER FELT BEFORE. JESUS
WILL COME IN AND BE WITH YOU
ALWAYS. YOU CAN CALL HIM ANY

TIME OF THE DAY OR NIGHT, JESUS IS NEVER BUSY. THINK FOR ONE MINUTE; WHAT IF THIS THING IS REAL? TRY IT, WHAT DO YOU HAVE TO LOSE? I TELL PEOPLE ALL THE TIME TO GET THE FACTS, BECAUSE THERE IS NO SECOND CHANCE ONCE YOU LEAVE THIS WORLD. SO THINK ABOUT IT LONG AND HARD. GIVE YOURSELF A SECOND CHANCE. ONE THING ABOUT HELL IS, THERE ARE NO UNBELIEVERS AND HELL IS NEVER FULL; **"SO DON'T HAVE A PLACE THERE."** GOD DOESN'T WISH NONE TO PERISH.

REVELATION 21:27 And there shall in no wise enter into it **any thing** that **defileth**, neither *whatsoever* worketh **abomination**, or *maketh* **a lie: but they which are written in the Lamb's book of life.**

2 Peter 3:7 But the heavens and the earth, which are now, by the same word are kept in store, **reserved unto fire against the day of judgment and perdition of ungodly men.**

2 Peter 3:9 The Lord is not slack concerning his promise, as some men count slackness; but is longsuffering to us-ward, **not willing that any should perish**, but that all should come to repentance.

PRAY FOR ONE ANOTHER, THAT ALL MEN WHO CALL ON THE NAME OF THE FATHER, SON AND HOLY SPIRIT; WILL BECOME A NEW CREATURE.

SANTIFICATION (CHAPTER 5)

SANTIFICATION: GOD'S CLEANSING PROCESS TO SEPARATE OR SET APART, MAKE ONE LIKE JESUS, "**THE REQUIREMENT IS TO BE BORN-AGAIN**".

2 Corinthians 7:1 Having therefore these promises, dearly beloved, **let us cleanse ourselves from all filthiness of the flesh and spirit, perfecting holiness in the fear of God.**

WHAT DOES GOD WANT FROM BELIEVERS? TO BE HOLY AND TO LOVE ONE ANOTHER. MANY CHURCHES TODAY, ARE DEAD WITH DEAD WORKS. WHEN I SPEAK OF THE CHURCH, I'M NOT TALKING ABOUT THE BUILDING; I'M TALKING ABOUT PEOPLE BEING BORN-AGAIN. FREE FROM THE PENALTY OF SIN. THOSE WHO KNOW JESUS AS THEIR

PERSONAL SAVIOR AND IS NOT
ASHAMED OR AFRAID TO TELL A
DYING WORLD; THAT JESUS LIVES
TODAY IN THE HEART OF MEN. AND
THAT JESUS IS ALIVE. THOSE WHO
ARE NOT AFRAID, TO LET THEIR LIGHT
SHINE IN A DARK PLACE. SOME
PEOPLE TODAY, CONFESS TO KNOW
JESUS, BUT THEIR HEART IS FAR
FROM HIM. THEY ARE BELIEVING IN
EVERY THING, EXCEPT **"JESUS CHRIST
AND HIM CRUCIFIED."** THE SPIRIT IS
DEAD IN MANY HEARTS TODAY. THEY
HAVE ADOPTED "**PSYCHOLOGY**"
OVER THE HOLY SPIRIT; THEY NO
LONGER LOOK TO THE SOURCE
"**(JESUS CHRIST)."** THEY LOOK TO
EVERY THING UNDER THE SUN THAT
IS GOING TO BENEFIT THEIR CAUSE,
ALWAYS MOVING IN THE WRONG
DIRECTION. SATAN HAS THEM
BLINDED TO THE THINGS OF THIS
WORLD. IN THE WORLD WE HAVE

ABORTION, GAMBLING AND IN
CERTAIN PARTS OF THE COUNTRY-
PROSITUTION, ETC... WHEN A
COUNTRY DOES NOT LIVE UNDER
GOD'S LAW, IT HAS BECOME
"LAWLESSNESS." MEANING THERE IS
SO MUCH CORRUPTION, IT IS NOT FIT
FOR BELIEVERS TO LIVE IN SUCH A
CORRUPT WORLD. WE SEE SO MUCH
KILLING, PEOPLE ARE AFRAID TO
SPEAK TO ONE ANOTHER. THINGS
HAVE CHANGED A LOT. IT IS LIKE THE
WORD OF GOD TELLS US IN THE LAST
DAYS; WE WILL NOT BE RECOGNIZED.
THE BELIEVER MUST KEEP HIS OR HER
SELF UNSPOTTED FROM THIS
WORLD. THIS IS THE CHURCH WE ARE
TALKING ABOUT, THERE ARE
BELIEVERS WHO HAVE LOST THEIR
WAY. THESE ARE PEOPLE, WHO
CONFESS TO KNOW JESUS CHRIST AS
LORD AND SAVIOR; BUT HAVE NEVER
BEEN BORN-AGAIN. ONE CAN'T SAY

THAT HE LOVES GOD AND HATE HIS BROTHER. THIS IS THE **"SANTIFICATION PROCESS"** THAT THE BELIEVER IN CHRIST BE PURE AND SANTIFIED FROM ALL UNRIGHTOUSNESS; CLEANSED BY THE BLOOD OF JESUS. THE BIBLE TELLS US TO BE NOT CONFORMED TO THIS WORLD. THE BELIEVER MUST KEEP HIS GARMENT PURE, CLEAN AND UNSPOTTED FROM "**THIS EVIL, AND ADULTEROUS WORLD."** SANTIFICATION TAKES PLACE IN THE HEART, NOT JUST THE MIND. SIN KEEPS THE MIND IN BONDAGE, BUT GOD SETS THE HEART FREE. WHEN YOU TRUST JESUS AS YOUR SAVIOR, ONLY JESUS CAN CLEANSE THE HEART. ONE CAN'T ENTER IN THE KINGDOM, YOU MUST BE BORN-AGAIN OF A **"MEEK HEART."** ONLY JESUS CAN MAKE THIS POSSIBLE BY THE WORD OF GOD. I SEE AND TALK

TO CHRISTIANS THAT DON'T HAVE
THE SANTIFICATION PROCESS IN
THEIR LIVES BECAUSE OF WHAT THEY
BELIEVE IN. MANY CHURCHES ARE
NOT TEACHING SANTIFICATION
BECAUSE MANY CHURCHES NO
LONGER BELIEVE IN THE HOLY SPIRIT.
THE SPIRIT IS NO LONGER IN OUR
CHURCHES TODAY. POLITICS HAS
GROWN TO BECOME THE TOPIC IN
MANY CHURCHES, INSTEAD OF THE
WORD OF GOD. THERE ARE STILL
SOME CHURCHES THAT THE HOLY
SPIRIT, STILL TEACHES IN. BUT DO
NOT ALLOW THE ENEMY TO DECEIVE
YOU, SO THAT THEY BECOME FEW IN
NUMBERS. SANTIFICATION IN THE
CHURCH TODAY, MANY CHURCHES
HAVE BOUGHT IN EVERY THING AND
HAS PUT THE WORD OF GOD OUT OF
THE CHURCH. JUST MAKE ME FEEL
GOOD. THE SEDUCING SPIRITS, AND
DOCTRINES OF DEVILS HAS ENTERED

THE CHURCH AND TAKEN OVER THE
MINDS OF MANY PEOPLE. THE
DECEIVED CHURCH IS NO LONGER
LOOKING TO THE SOURCE "**(JESUS
CHRIST)."** THE DECEIVED CHURCH
HAS CAST THEIR FIRST LOVE OFF; THE
BIBLE TELL US, MANY SHALL DEPART
FROM THE FAITH THAT IS IN THE
BLOOD OF JESUS CHRIST. THE
SEDUCING SPIRITS ARE RUNNING
MANY CHURCHES TODAY; THAT'S
THE REASON MANY MEN'S HEARTS
ARE FAINTING. THERE IS A LACK OF
TRUTH BEING TAUGHT ANYMORE.
THE NEW SLOGAN OF MANY
CHURCHES SEEMS TO BE, "JUST
FOLLOW YOUR HEART, AND THAT
WILL TELL YOU WHAT IS RIGHT OR
WRONG." MANY PEOPLE DO NOT
WANT TO HEAR THE TRUTH. IT'S ALL
ABOUT ME, MYSELF AND I; BUT
WHERE IS GOD? IT IS SAD THE
CONDITION MANY HEARTS ARE IN.

ASK GOD TO SHOW YOU THE TRUTH,
THE GOD OF ABRAHAM, ISSAC, AND
JACOB; WILL GUIDE YOU INTO ALL
TRUTH. THE TRUTH SHALL MAKE YOU
FREE. LET THE CHAINS FALL OFF
YOUR SOUL, SO YOU CAN BE FREE TO
SERVE GOD. HE (GOD) IS CALLING,
COME HOME. COME HOME TO THE
OUT STRETCHED ARMS OF THE LORD,
THAT THE ANGELS MAY REJOICE
OVER ONE SINNER. PEOPLE NEED TO
SEE CHRIST IN US FIRST, BEFORE THEY
WILL WANT TO GIVE THEIR HEART TO
CHRIST. GOD STILL HAVE SOLIDERS IN
THE CHURCH THAT IS FAITHFUL; THE
WHOLE CHURCH IS NOT FILLED WITH
"**UNBELIEF.**" MANY MAY BELIEVE
THAT JESUS IS DEAD AND STILL IN
THE GRAVE; BUT GOD HAS RAISED
JESUS FROM THE GRAVE. MANY
PEOPLE THESE DAYS, DON'T BELIEVE
IN HELL. THEY THINK BECAUSE THEY
ARE UNDER GRACE, AND NOT THE

LAW THAT GOD WORD HAS
"**CHANGED.**" JESUS CAME ONLY TO
"**FULFILL**" THE LAW, AND THAT WAS
TO BRING MAN UNTO CHRIST.
TODAY, WE WALK BY FAITH AND
FAITH ALONE. WE CAN'T ADD
NOTHING OR TAKE AWAY ANYTHING
FROM THE CROSS. THE BIBLE SAYS IF
WE ADD, GOD WILL ADD THE
PLAGUES UNTO HIM. IF WE TAKE
AWAY, GOD WILL BLOT OUT OUR
NAME FROM THE BOOK OF LIFE. THE
"**SANTIFICATION PROCESS**" IS A
DAILY PROCESS THAT BEGINS WHEN
THE BELIEVER FIRST GIVES HIS OR
HER LIFE TO CHRIST. WE NO LONGER
LIVE THE LIFE WE ONCE LIVED, WE
ARE NOW A NEW CREATURE IN
CHRIST, WE HAVE PUT OFF THE OLD
MAN (THE DEEDS OF THE WORLD,
LUST, LYINGING, STEALING, ETC)., WE
HAVE BECOME A WHOLE DIFFERENT
PERSON. NOW YOU MUST GROW IN

GRACE, AND YOU CAN'T DO THIS ON YOUR OWN (STRENGTH). CHRIST MUST BE THE CENTER OF YOUR LIFE. THIS IS A DIFFICULT TASK FOR THE BELIEVER ON THEIR OWN, BECAUSE THE FLESH MUST BE **"CRUCIFIED."** AND ONLY CHRIST CAN DO THE WORK THAT IS NEEDED IN OUR LIFE. REMEMBER ALL GOOD AND RIGHTEOUS THINGS COME FROM ABOVE. EVERYTHING WE HAVE, GOD DID IT OR GAVE IT TO US. EVERY CHRISTIAN WILL FAIL, PAUL EVEN FAILED BECAUSE HE DIDN'T KNOW OR UNDERSTAND THE WORD OF GOD. **"EXAMPLE,"** I CAN'T EVEN RAISE MY ARM WITHOUT GOD. UNTIL THE BELIEVER KNOWS AND UNDERSTANDS THIS, HE WILL FAIL EVERY TIME. WE CAN'T DO ANYTHING WITHOUT GOD, THAT'S THE REASON WE NEED THE HOLY SPIRIT. EVERY BELIEVER POSSESSES

THE HOLY SPIRIT. YOU MUST ALLOW
THE HOLY SPIRIT TO LEAD YOU IN,
ACCORDING TO GOD'S WORD. THIS
WAS PAUL'S PROBLEM. REMEMBER,
WE SAID THAT THE FLESH MUST BE
CRUCIFIED; WITHOUT THE FLESH
BEING CRUCIFIED, YOU ARE WALKING
BY YOURSELF. AND THAT IS FAILURE
IN THE FLESH. PAUL ALSO WAS
BAPTIZED WITH THE HOLY SPIRIT;
THIS IS ANOTHER SUBJECT, THE
BAPTISMAL OF THE HOLY SPIRIT. THE
POINT I'M MAKING IS, JESUS IS THE
AUTHOR OF OUR FAITH, AND IF WE
PUT OUR TRUST IN ANYTHING OTHER
THAN **"CHRIST AND HIM CRUCIFIED,"**
WE ARE HEADED FOR TROUBLE. YOU
CAN HAVE ALL THE GIFTS OF THE
SPIRIT, IT DOES NOT MATTER.
WITHOUT THE HOLY SPIRIT, YOU
WILL **"FAIL"** TIME AFTER TIME.
THAT'S THE REASON YOU SEE SO
MANY CHRISTIANS THAT DO NOT

HAVE VICTORY IN THEIR LIVES. THEY
PRAY AND PRAY, DO EVERYTHING IN
THEIR POWER AND IT ONLY LEADS TO
MORE **"FAILURE."** BECAUSE THEY
FAIL TO LOOK TO THE SOURCE
"(JESUS CHRIST)." THIS IS A LESSON
FOR ALL BELIEVERS, NO ONE HAS
EVER WENT FROM THE SIXTH
CHAPTER OF ROMANS; TO THE
EIGHTH CHAPTER, BEFORE MAKING A
STOP IN THE **"SEVENTH CHAPTER."**
**("READ CHAPTERS 6-8 OF
ROMANS").** YOU WILL BEGAN TO
UNDERSTAND THAT YOU NEED JESUS
TO HOLD YOUR HAND. WE CAN DO
NOTHING WITHOUT THE CROSS, WE
MUST KEEP OUR FOCUS ON THE
CROSS. THAT IS WHAT KEEPS SATAN,
AND THE WORLD FROM TAKING
OVER THIS WORLD. IT WAS THE
CROSS THAT DEFEATED HIM
"(SATAN)." THE POWER LIES IN JESUS
AND JESUS ONLY, SO BEFORE YOU

ATTEMPT TO MAKE A MOVE REMEMBER IT TAKES THE CROSS TO GAIN VICTORY; ONLY IN JESUS WILL YOU FIND PEACE. FOR HE IS "**THE PRINCE OF PEACE.**" HE (JESUS) WILL NOT LEAD YOU DOWN THE WRONG PATH, BUT WILL GUIDE YOU INTO ALL TRUTH; FOR JESUS IS TRUTH. THERE IS NO OTHER NAME, WHERE MAN CAN BE SAVED. TRUST HIM TO LEAD AND GUIDE YOU THROUGH THE SANTIFICATION PROCESS. IT IS VITAL IN YOUR LIFE. WITHOUT IT, YOU WILL RETURN TO THE THINGS YOU USED TO DO; NEVER COMING TO "**THE KNOWLEDGE OF CHRIST.**" REMEMBER, THE FLESH MUST BE CRUCIFIED BEFORE YOU CAN BEGIN THE WORK CHRIST HAS FOR YOU.

WHY DOES SATAN HATE THE CROSS (CHAPTER 6)

THE CROSS IS WHAT **"DEFEATED HIM"** (SATAN). THE CHURCH HAS ITS FAITH IN A LOT OF THINGS; PREACHING, TEACHING, SINGING, TITHING, BEST OUFIT, MONEY, POSITION IN THE CHURCH OR THIS IS MY SEAT (I HAVE BEEN SITTING HERE FOR FORTY-YEARS), ETC…, WHAT IS THE MAIN THING WE SHOULD BE CONCERNED ABOUT? WE SHOULD BE CONCERNED MORE ABOUT ONE ANOTHER; INSTEAD OF THINGS THAT HAVE NO VALUE TO THE CROSS. THOSE THINGS ARE GOOD IN THEIR OWN WAY, WE NEED ALL OF THOSE THINGS TO OPERATE THE CHURCH; AS WELL AS OUR LIVES. OUR

LIVES SHOULD NOT CONSIST IN
THE THINGS WE HAVE, BUT
SHOULD CONSIST SOLELY IN
THE LORD. IF WE LOVE THE
WORLD, THE LOVE OF GOD IS
NOT IN US. WE MUST BE
CARFUL OF THE THINGS WE
TAKE FOR GRANTED, OUR SOUL
DEPENDS ON THE THINGS WE
TAKE TO THE CROSS. AND NOT
THE THINGS WE TEND TO WANT
TO LOVE SO MUCH MORE,
THAN GOD. YES, I SAID THE
THINGS OF GOD. WE SHOULD
PRAY TO THE FATHER BEFORE
WE CLAIM ANY THING
BECAUSE IT ALL BELONGS TO
THE LORD. WE ARE JUST
BORROWING THE THINGS THAT
GOD HAS TRUSTED US WITH.
CAN GOD TRUST YOU WITH THE
THINGS YOU HAVE? IF GOD
CAN TRUST YOU, THEN YOU
SHOULD BE **"SATISFIED."** I

WATCH PEOPLE PLAY WITH
THEIR TOYS, THEY BECOME
IDOLS INSTEAD OF BLESSINGS.
MANY CHURCHES (THE WORLD)
HAVE TRADED THE CROSS; FOR
RELIGION, PSYCHOLOGY,
ETC…, GOD HAS GIVEN HIS
CHILDREN WHAT THEY NEED.
PEOPLE STILL GAMBLE ON
IDOLS, BECAUSE THEY ARE
STILL TRYING TO FILL A VOID
IN THEIR LIVES. I'VE LEARNED
TO CHANGE THE THINGS I CAN,
AND ACCEPT THE THINGS I
CAN'T CHANGE. THE FIRST
THING PEOPLE SAY IS, "I'M
TRYING TO HELP MY FAMILY
OR FRIENDS." WHICH IS NOT
ALWAYS TRUE. YOU MUCH
SEARCH YOUR SOUL FOR THE
TRUTH, AND NOT LET A LIE
CONSUME YOU. YOU SEE, IT
ONLY LEADS TO NEEDING
MORE TOYS. YOU MAY EVEN

START THINKING THEY ARE YOUR GOD. YOU MAY BE TEMPTED TO START LOOKING TO THEM, INSTEAD OF GOD. I LIKE THAT SAYING, NOBODY WANTS YOU WHEN YOU ARE DOWN AND OUT; THAT IS A TRUE SAYING. SATAN HATES YOU TITHING- **"WHY?"** BECAUSE THE CURSE IS LIFTED, GOD WILL REBUKE THE DEVOURER (SATAN); THE FRUITS OF YOUR LABOR SHALL BE BLESSED, I DARE YOU TO TRY HIM. YES, SATAN WILL COME TO YOU WHEN YOU HAVE BUILT UP SOME EQUITY. WHAT I MEAN IS, AFTER A FEW YEARS, SATAN WILL ATTEMPT TO SHOW YOU HOW MUCH MONEY YOU COULD HAVE; IF YOU WERE NOT GIVING IT TO THE LORD, FOR HIS (LORD) KINGDOM. SO MANY

CHRISTIANS HAVE MADE THIS MISTAKE, OF BUILDING A HOUSE WITHOUT "**A FOUNDATION.**" THIS IS A DISASTER WAITING TO HAPPEN.

PSALMS 127:1 A Song of degrees for Solomon. Except the LORD build the **house,** they labour in vain that build it: except the LORD keep the city, **the watchman waketh *but in vain.***

SO MANY CHRISTIANS HAVE FALLEN INTO THE TRAP, THAT SATAN HAS DECEIVED THEM IN BELIEVING. HE DECEIVES THEM INTO BELIEVING THEY CAN GAIN THE WHOLE WORLD. NO CHRISTIAN SETS OUT ON THIS PATH, BUT FINDS HIM OR HERSELF ON THE ROAD OF DESTRUCTION. **"YES, DESTRUCTION."** WE SHOULD ONLY TAKE WHAT GOD GIVES US, BECAUSE GREATER IS HE THAT IS IN YOU, THAN HE THAT IS IN THE WORLD. IF MAN WILL LOOK ONLY TO

THE CROSS, HE WILL BE LIKE A TREE PLANTED BY THE RIVERS OF WATER. THE CROSS IS NOT BEING PREACHED AS MUCH TODAY. IN MANY CHURCHES, MANY PEOPLE MAY BE LOOKING TO THE PREACHER, PSYCHOLOGY, PSYCHICS, PSYCHIATRY, ETC., DO NOT TAKE YOUR EYES OFF THE CROSS. IT IS EASY TO TAKE YOUR EYES OFF THE CROSS AND START BELIEVING IN OTHER THINGS; THAT ONLY PERTAIN TO THE FLESH. SATAN USES THESE TOOLS TO GUDE AND CONTROL PEOPLE. IN THE CROSS, YOUR SANTIFICATION PROCESS WILL STOP; IF THIS HAS HAPPENED TO YOU. YOU CAN'T SERVE TWO MASTERS AT THE SAME TIME; ONE WILL HATE THE OTHER OR DESPISE THE OTHER. THIS DOES NOT MEAN THAT YOU HAVE LOST YOUR SALVATION, IT JUST MEANS YOU HAVE WENT DOWN THE WRONG

PATH AND YOU ARE "**LISTENING**" TO THE WRONG SPIRIT. MANY PEOPLE BELIEVE THEY ARE DOING THE RIGHT THING MOST OF THE TIME, BECAUSE WHEN WE LEAN TO OUR OWN UNDERSTANDING; GOD'S MESSAGES CAN'T GET TO OUR EARS. ALTHOUGH, EVERYTHING MAY SEEM RIGHT TO US IN OUR EYE SIGHT; WE MUST ALWAYS LOOK TO GOD FOR INSTRUCTION AND GUIDANCE IN OUR LIFE. GOD IS NOT GOING TO FORSAKE US, GOD LOVES US TO MUCH. GOD KNOWS THE ENEMY BECAUSE GOD CREATED SATAN "(**PERFECT IN BEAUTY),**" BEFORE SATAN AND ONE-THIRD OF THE ANGELS WERE KICKED OUT OF HEAVEN. "**INQUITY**" WAS FOUND IN HIM (SATAN), THAT'S THE REASON SATAN WANTS TO DESTROY EVERY THING THAT GOD HAS FOR YOU. SATAN WANTS TO BE GOD, TO

CONTROL THIS WORLD, AND GOD'S
PEOPLE. GOD IS GOING TO DESTROY
SATAN IN THE END, AND ALL OF
THEM THAT (WORSHIP) SATAN. YOU
CAN'T BEGAN TO SERVE GOD, UNTIL
YOU KNOW THE "**ENEMY.**" IF YOU
DO NOT KNOW THE ENEMY, YOU
WILL BLAME GOD FOR WHAT THE
ENEMY HAS DONE; NOT KNOWING
THE DIFFERENCE IN THEIR WORK.
YOU NEED TO KNOW THE STRATEGY
OF SATAN, TO BE ABLE TO DISCERN
WHAT IS GOOD FROM WHAT IS EVIL.
SATAN WORKS IN THE "**MIND**" OF
MAN, BECAUSE THAT IS WHERE MAN
IS THE WEAKEST. REMEMBER, HE
DECEIVED EVE IN THE GARDEN OF
EDEN, AND IT LED TO AN ATTACK ON
HER MIND. SATAN GOT EVE TO
"**DOUBT**" WHAT GOD HAD TOLD HER.
SATAN DECEIVED HER AND EVE
DECEIVED ADAM, HER HUSBAND. WE
MUST HAVE THE WORD OF GOD IN

FRONT OF US, TO BE ABLE TO DEFEAT
THE ENEMY AND THAT IS THE
"**CROSS.**" NEVER TAKE YOUR EYES
OFF OF JESUS, IT ONLY LEADS TO
FAILURE. SATAN IS VERY CUNNING;
MAN IS THE SAME WAY. BE CAREFUL
OF WHAT YOU "**SEE AND HEAR.**" IF
IT'S NOT THE WORD OF GOD, RUN!
(GET AWAY AND DON'T LISTEN). IT IS
ONLY THE ENEMY TRYING TO GET A
FOOTHOLD IN YOUR LIFE. WE MUST
BE ROOTED DOWN IN THE WORD OF
GOD BEFORE WE CAN EVEN BEGIN
THIS JOURNEY. THIS JOURNEY
REQUIRES DISCIPLINE. YOU MUST
LEARN TO OBEY EVERY WORD THAT
PROCEEDETH OUT OF MOUTH OF
GOD. ONLY THEN WILL YOU BE ABLE
TO PUT ON THE WHOLE ARMOUR OF
GOD. THAT'S THE REASON, SO MANY
CHRISTIANS ARE EXPERIENCING
TROUBLE, IN THEIR EVERY DAY WALK
WITH CHRIST. THE WORD OF GOD IS

THE MOST IMPORTANT THING IN OUR LIFE. WE ARE TO SEEK GOD'S KINGDOM FIRST, AND GOD'S RIGHTEOUSNESS FOR OUR LIVES. WE ARE TO GO TO GOD FOR THE ANSWERS TO OUR PROBLEMS IN LIFE, BEFORE WE MAKE ANY MOVES THAT LEAD US, TOWARDS OUR OWN PATHS OF RIGHTEOUSNESS. SAD TO SAY, MOST CHRISTIANS DON'T HAVE THE WORD OF GOD IN THEIR LIVES, TO GUIDE THEM IN THEIR LIFE. THEY THINK THEY ARE DOING THE RIGHT THING, UNTIL THE PROBLEM GETS BIGGER THAN THE SITUATION. WE CAN'T PUT OUR SEEDS ON THE **"WAY SIDE, THRONES, OR STONY PLACES"**, WE MUST PLANT UPON **"GOOD GROUND,"** SO THE WORD OF GOD CAN BE RICH AND MULTIPLY IN OUR LIFE; SO THAT WE BRING NOT SHAME TO GOD. FOR CHRIST LIVES IN OUR HEART, AND WE ARE TO BE PLEASING

TO THE FATHER. GUARD YOUR MIND
AND HEART, THAT YOU WALK DAILY
WITH CHRIST. PRAY THAT YOUR
MIND BE RENEWED, FROM
MORNING TO MORNING; LOOKING
FOR THAT BLESSED HOPE THAT IS IN
YOU. YOU MUST TRAIN YOUR MIND
TO HEAR THE WORDS OF THE HOLY
SPIRIT. WHEN I SAY TRAIN, THAT
MEANS TO **"LISTEN"** TO THE WORD
OF GOD; AND ALLOW HIM TO
"INSTRUCT" YOU IN ALL AREAS OF
YOUR LIFE. GOD HAS GIVEN US GIFTS
TO SERVE HIM (GOD). YOU MUST
FIND YOUR GIFT AND START SERVING
GOD. DON'T TRY TO DO THE THINGS
GOD HAS NOT CALLED YOU TO DO,
THAT LEADS ONLY TO THE PATH OF
SATAN. SATAN WILL TRY TO GET YOU
OUTSIDE OF THE WILL OF GOD, BY
CREATING IN YOU, A DESIRE FOR
YOUR OWN WILL TO BE DONE. AND
THAT IS A BAD MOVE.

MANY BELIEVERS ARE CAUGHT UP IN
THIS TODAY, BECAUSE THEY WANTED
TO BE SOMETHING THAT GOD DID
NOT GIVE THEM. AND THIS IS CALLED
"**COVETING.**" THIS SIN WILL LEAD
YOU DOWN A DARK PATH. IF YOU
ARE ON THIS TRAIN GET OFF
"**(JUMP).**" IT ONLY LEADS TO
"**DESTRUCTION,**" WHICH IS "**DEATH.**"
SATAN WANTS YOU TO BELIEVE A LIE,
TO KEEP YOU IN SIN. WE ARE NOT TO
LIE TO ONE ANOTHER AS BELIEVERS.
THE WORLD DOES THAT BECAUSE
THEY WEAR A MASK MOST OF THE
TIME, TRYING TO BE SOMETHING
THAT THEY ARE NOT. YOU DON'T
HAVE TO PROVE ANYTHING TO GOD,
JUST KEEP YOUR EARS AND EYES
OPEN; TO RECEIVE THE THINGS GOD
HAS FOR YOU. KEEP IN MIND THE
WORLD DOES NOT LOVE YOU
ENOUGH TO TELL YOU THE TRUTH.
WITHOUT THE TRUTH YOU ARE LOST;

BECAUSE THE TRUTH IS THE ONLY THING WE HAVE TO STAND ON. WE ARE WALKING BY FAITH AND BELIEVING GOD'S WORD, IS GOING TO DO WHAT GOD SAYS THAT IT WILL DO. THIS IS HARD FOR MAN, BECAUSE THE SPIRIT OF GOD DOES NOT DWELL IN HIS HEART. THEREFORE, IT IS IMPOSSIBLE FOR HIM TO BELIEVE THE WORD OF GOD. LET GOD DO THE WORK IN YOUR LIFE; SO THAT YOU WILL BE PLEASING IN HIS (GOD'S) SIGHT. THE ONLY WAY IS THE **"SANTIFICATION PROCESS,"** THAT WILL MAKE YOU WHOLE.

THE AX IS LAID (CHAPTER 7)

SOMETIMES THE TREE JUST NEEDS TO BE PURNED, A LIMB HERE AND A LIMB THERE. THE BRANCH **("BELIEVER")** IS GOING TO NEED SUN LIGHT, WATER, AND CARING FROM THE VINE **("JESUS").** THE BRANCH **("BELIEVER"),** CAN'T BEAR FRUIT OF IT SELF, IT HAS TO ABIDE IN THE VINE **("JESUS").** WITHOUT THE CARE GIVER, THE BRANCH WOULD DIE AND BE CAST INTO THE FIRE. GOD EXPECTS US TO BRING FORTH FRUIT. HOW DO WE, AS GOD'S CHILDREN, BRING FORTH FRUIT? BY THE WORD OF GOD IN OUR LIFE. BY TRUSTING IN HIS WORD AND MEDITATING ON THE WORD OF GOD. THE BIBLE TELLS US IN...

John 15:7 If ye abide in me, and my **words** abide in you, ye shall ask what ye will, and it shall be done unto you.

IN TODAY'S SOCIETY, WILL MAN TURN TO GOD? AND ALSO, WILL MAN TURN BACK TO GOD? THE CHURCH IS WOUNDED, IT'S GOING TO TAKE GOD, TO BRING THE CHURCH BACK TO WHERE IT SHOULD BE. FOR THERE IS A FAMINE IN THE LAND FOR THE WORD OF GOD. MOSES, WAS INSTRUCTED BY GOD TO LEAD THE CHILDREN THROUGH THE RED SEA. GOD GAVE THEM LIFE, AS THEY PASSED THROUGH THE RED SEA. THE LORD WAS THEIR SHIELD OF PROTECTION AND THE LORD WATCHED OVER THEM AS THEY ALL CROSSED OVER. THE LORD WAS THEIR STRENGTH, AS THEY PASSED. GOD HELD

BACK PHARAOH FROM
DESTROYING THE CHILDREN OF
ISRAEL. GOD HARDENED
PHARAOH'S HEART, SO THAT
HE WOULD FOLLOW THE
CHILDREN OF ISRAEL; TO SHOW
THE EGYPTIANS, THAT **"I AM"**
THE LORD. THIS LESSON WAS
TO BE TAUGHT TO OTHER
NATIONS, THAT THERE WAS A
GOD AMONG HIS PEOPLE; AND
THAT NOTHING WAS TOO HARD
FOR GOD. NO ONE COMES IN
CONTACT WITH GOD AND
REMAINS THE SAME. PHARAOH
HAD TO LEARN A LESSON THAT
WOULD TEACH HIM THAT GOD
IS **"I AM."** GOD ALLOWS HIS
PEOPLE TO GO THROUGH THE
STORM; TO REFINE THEM AND
MOLD THEM FOR HIS USE. THE
CHILDREN CONTINUED TO
MURMUR AND TO REBEL
AGAINST GOD. THEY HAD NO

FAITH THAT GOD WOULD SEE
THEM THROUGH. MOSES HAD
TO CALM THEM OF THEIR
FEARS; THEY STILL CONTINUED
TO COMPLAIN AND WORRY
MOSES. THEY BELIEVED NOT
ON THE WORD OF THE LORD,
THAT **"I AM."** GOD HELD THE
EGYPTIANS BACK, WHILE THE
CHILDREN OF ISRAEL CROSSED
OVER. THERE WAS A CLOUD
BETWEEN THEM, UNTIL THE
CHILDREN OF ISRAEL REACHED
THE OTHER SIDE. I KNOW YOU
SAW THE SCENE IN THE MOVIE,
WHERE PHARAOH WAS
WATCHING FROM HIS
CARRIAGE, BUT THAT WAS THE
MOVIES. THE REAL DEAL WAS
THAT PHARAOH AND HIS ARMY
WAS DROWNED IN THE RED
SEA). THEY WERE LED BY THE
SPIRIT TO GO AFTER THE
CHILDREN OF ISRAEL. GOD HAD

TO SHOW THE EGYPTIANS AND
THE NATIONS THAT HE IS **"I
AM."** THE CHILDREN OF ISRAEL
DRANK OF THAT **"ROCK"**,
WHICH WAS **"CHRIST"** GOD'S
SON, THE ROCK TYPIFIED
CHRIST. **IN EXODUS 14:31,** THE
CHILDREN OF ISRAEL SAW THE
GREAT WORK THAT THE LORD
DID UPON THE EGYPTIANS. AND
THE PEOPLE FEARED THE LORD,
AND BELIEVED THE LORD. AND
HIS SERVANT MOSES, PHARAOH
AND HIS ARMY THOUGHT THEY
COULD DESTROY GOD'S
PEOPLE, BUT GOD ALWAYS
TAKES CARE OF HIS PEOPLE.
EVEN TODAY, GOD IS STILL **"I
AM."** IF YOU ARE IN DOUBT,
WATCH THE LORD AT WORK.
FOR MOST OR MANY OF THEM,
GOD WAS NOT PLEASED WITH
THEIR ATTITUDES. THEY
STARTED BACK COMPLAINING,

FORGETTING **"I AM"** THE GOD
THAT BROUGHT THEM OUT OF
EGYPT. THE CHILDREN OF
ISRAEL WAS REBELLIOUS IN
THE WILDERNESS, AGAINST
MOSES AND AGAINST GOD.
THE CHILDREN OF GOD IN THE
WILDERNESS, REBELLED
AGAINST GOD TO THE POINT
THAT GOD HAD TO LET THEM
WANDER IN THE WILDERNESS
FOR **"FORTY-YEARS"** BEFORE
HE COULD RID THE SIN IN THE
CAMP. ONLY JOSHUA AND
CALEB WERE ALLOWED TO
REACH THE PROMISE LAND.
THESE WERE THE CHILDREN OF
ISRAEL THAT CAME THROUGH
THE RED SEA. PEOPLE BELIEVE
THIS; GOD IS NOT GOING TO
DEAL WITH NO SIN, ONLY THE
"PURE IN HEART" WILL SEE
GOD. THERE IS NO VICTORY IN

DEATH, ONLY
"DESTRUCTION".

AMOS 8:11 Behold, the days come, saith the Lord GOD, that I will send a famine in the land, not a famine of bread, nor a thirst for water, **but of hearing the words of the LORD:**

THIS IS NOT FOR BELIEVERS, BUT FOR THOSE OUTSIDE OF THE CHURCH. GOD IS NOT TALKING ABOUT THE BUILDING, BUT THEIR RELATIONSHIP WITH JESUS CHRIST. SOME PEOPLE THINK THAT IT'S OK TO SAY, "I'M DOING THE BEST I CAN." WE MUST LOOK TO GOD FOR THE STRENGTH WE NEED; NOT DEPEND ON OUR OWN ABILITY. OUR OWN ABILITY DOES NOT ALLOW US TO DEPEND ON GOD. THE PROBLEM IS THE **PRONOUN I.** ALL MAN NEEDS IS: GOD'S LOVE, MERCY, AND GRACE. I THANK GOD FOR HIS MERCY AND GRACE; IT HAS SUSTAINED ME DURING THE YEARS AND GRACE WILL

LED ME HOME. MAN THINKS HE HAS A LOT OF TIME TO GET IT TOGETHER. UNLESS GOD DRAWS HIM OR HER, THEY WILL NOT MAKE IT IN THE KINGDOM OF HEAVEN. YOU MUST ACCEPT JESUS CHRIST AS YOUR PERSONAL SAVIOR AND LORD. GIVE YOUR LIFE TO THE KING FOR HE (JESUS) IS THE ONE WHO WILL SAVE YOU FROM YOUR SINS. JESUS PAID THE SIN DEBT FOR ALL OF US; A DEBT THAT WE COULD NOT PAY FOR OURSELVES. SATAN HAD US BOUND IN BONDAGE, BUT THE CROSS FREED US, NOW WE (BELIEVERS) WILL GO TO BE WITH THE LORD, AFTER DEATH. IF YOU WILL JUST TRUST JESUS, HE WILL MAKE IT ALRIGHT FOR YOU. YOU WILL BE LIKE PURE GOLD, THAT HAS BEEN REFINED. HIS MERCY IS RENEWED EVERY MORNING; HE PROTECTS HIS CHILDREN FROM THIS CORRUPT

WORLD. HE PLANTS EVERY TREE
WHERE THE FRUIT CAN GROW, THE
HEAT DOES NOT SCORCH THE TREE,
THE WATER DOES NOT SHEAR THE
BARK FROM THE TREE. THE SON
(JESUS) CARES FOR ALL WHO ARE IN
THE CROSS, FOR THEY TRUST NOT IN
THEMSELVES TO BRING FORTH FRUIT.
THEIR FRUIT WAS ACCEPTED UNTO
THE LORD SOME 30 FOLD, SOME 60
FOLD AND SOME 100 FOLD. IF YOU
TRY TO DO THIS ON YOUR OWN, YOU
WILL FAIL AND BE CAST IN THE FIRE.
YOU MUST REPENT OF YOUR SINS,
TURN TO THE SOURCE (JESUS), FOR
HE CARES FOR YOU. HE WILL NEVER
LEAVE YOU OR FORSAKE YOU. YOUR
TREE WILL NEVER DIE, IT WILL HAVE
MORE FRUIT TO SHARE WITH
FRIENDS AND FAMILY. THE WILLFUL
LIFE (SHARING), AND YOUR FAMILY IS
WHAT GOD CALLS A CHEERFUL
GIVER. HE (JESUS) WILL BRING

ABUNDANCE TO YOUR LIFE, MEANING **PLENTY.** IF YOU HAVE TWO COATS, GIVE ONE TO A FRIEND IN NEED. FOR WE ARE ALL BROTHERS, REGARDLESS OF OUR SKIN COLOR. GIVE AND YE SHALL RECEIVE FROM THE LORD, DON'T BE LIKE ANANIAS AND SAPPHIRA (HIS WIFE); WHO SOLD THEIR POSSESSIONS AND KEPT BACK PART OF THE MONEY. THEY LIED TO THE HOLY SPIRIT. THE BIBLE TELLS US NOT TO LIE TO ONE ANOTHER. THE POSSESSIONS THEY HAD WERE NOT THEIR OWN, BUT ALL THINGS COMMON; MEANING THEY WERE ALL TO BE AS ONE, SHARING AND CARING FOR ONE ANOTHER. MAN'S PROBLEM IS HIS GREED AND SELFISHNESS. HE WANTS EVERYTHING FOR HIMSELF. A PERSON CAN HAVE A 100,000,000 DOLLARS AND YOU CAN BE MAKING 8 TO 12 DOLLARS AN HOUR; HE OR

SHE WILL STEAL FROM YOU, AND
LEAVE ONLY THE CRUMBS.

**READ THE STORY THE RICH MAN
AND LAZARUS, LUKE 16:19-31.**

IT HAPPENS TO US EVERYDAY, WHEN
WE THINK WE HAVE AN EXTRA
DOLLAR, SOME FIND A WAY TO STEAL
IT FROM US. CONTENTMENT ONLY
COMES FROM THE LORD. THERE ARE
ONLY TWO TYPES OF PEOPLE IN THIS
WORLD; AND THAT'S GIVERS AND
TAKERS. IT'S ONLY IN THE CROSS
THAT MAN WILL FIND THE FRUIT OF
THE SPIRIT. WHAT MAKES MAN THE
WAY HE IS? "**GREED.**" HE CAN'T GET
ENOUGH. HE OR SHE DOES NOT
WANT TO WORK FOR WHAT THEY
WANT; INSTEAD THEY FIND A WAY
TO TAKE IT. OUR SOCIETY HAS BEEN
TAUGHT TO BEG INSTEAD OF
WORKING FOR WHAT YOU WANT
AND IT IS SAD MANY PEOPLE ARE

THIS WAY. FOR EXAMPLE, OUR CITIES ARE FILTHY BECAUSE PEOPLE WON'T BEND OVER TO PICK UP A PIECE OF PAPER ON THE GROUND. SOME OF THE MEN THAT HAVE A LAWN SERVICE; LEAVE THE GRASS ON THE SIDE WALKS, STREET, AND EVEN IN THE YARDS. THEY WANT THE MONEY, BUT NOT THE WORK. THERE HAVE BEEN MANY PEOPLE TO ASK ME TO WORK FOR THEM, I TELL THEM WHAT I CAN DO, BEFORE I START WORK. IF THEY WANT ME TO TAKE A SHORT CUT (HALF DO THE JOB) I TELL THEM NO, REGARDLESS OF THE MONEY. BECAUSE I HAVE TO BE PLEASING TO THE LORD AND GOD SEES ALL THAT WE DO. WE SHOULD ALWAYS DO OUR BEST. REMEMBER, WE ARE ALL UNDER "**TALENTS.**" THE AX IS LAID TO EVERY MAN'S TREE, SO BE CAREFUL WHAT YOU SAY AND DO, THE FATHER SEES ALL. WE ARE TO DO

OUR BEST IN EVERY THING WE DO. I
PRAY THAT THE LORD WILL BRING
OUR SOCIETY BACK TO INTEGRITY;
THAT THE WORD OF GOD WILL HAVE
A PLACE IN THE HEART OF MAN. YOU
CAN'T DO THIS WITHOUT TALENTS,
YOU HAVE TO BE TAUGHT THE WORD
OF GOD. THE BIBLE SAYS IF A MAN
DOESN'T WORK, NEITHER DOES HE
EAT. MAN NEEDS TO COME BACK TO
GOD FOR DIRECTION IN HIS OR HER
LIFE. TRYING TO DO THIS ON YOUR
OWN WILL ONLY CAUSE YOU MORE
PAIN AND DISAPPOINTMENT. SO
GIVE YOUR TIME AND TALENTS SO
GOD CAN LEAD YOU OUT OF
BONDAGE. LET THE ENEMY GO, AND
LET GOD.

THE BRANCH IS THE **("BELEIVER").** IN
ORDER TO BRING FORTH FRUIT, WE
MUST PLANT SEEDS FOR CHRIST. THE
SEEDS WE PLANT DETERMINES WHAT
FRUIT WE BARE IN OUR LIVES. WHEN

GOD WATERS THOSE SEEDS, IT BRINGS FORTH MORE FRUIT. FOR OUR FRUIT TO BARE MORE FRUIT, WE MUST LOOK TO JESUS **("VINE").** LOOK AT MANY CHRISTIANS TODAY, THEY HAVE NO FRUIT IN THEIR LIVES. THEN HOW CAN THEY BE CHRISTIANS? WELL, THIS IS CALLED LUKE WARM CHRISTIANS, THAT ARE NEITHER HOT OR COLD. THEY DO VERY LITTLE FOR THE KINGDOM. THEY GO ABOUT EVERY DAY LIFE, WITHOUT A CARE OR CONCERN FOR THE KINGDOM OF GOD. THEY HAVE LOST THEIR WAY FROM THE LOVE OF CHRIST AND HIS MERCY BUT THEY CAN STILL COME BACK TO GOD; THEY JUST NEED TO REPENT AND START BEARING FRUIT. YOU CAN'T JUST GET SAVED AND THAT'S IT. WE ARE TO BECOME DISCIPLES FOR CHRIST AND TO LEAD OTHERS TO CHRIST. THERE ARE SO MANY CHRISTIANS THAT

HAVE NEVER LED ANY ONE TO CHRIST. WHEN I SAY LED, I MEAN THEY ARE AFRAID TO TALK TO PEOPLE ABOUT CHRIST. SOME DON'T EVEN KNOW HOW TO LEAD A SINNER TO CHRIST. WE MUST STUDY OUR BIBLES AND DEVELOP A PERSONAL RELATIONSHIP WITH GOD. SOME MAY SAY, "AT MY CHURCH, THE PREACHER IS NOT TEACHING THE WORD OF GOD; SO IT IS THE PREACHER'S FAULT THAT I CAN NOT WITNESS TO ANYBODY." EVERY CHRISTIAN SHOULD BE ABLE TO LEAD SOMEONE TO CHRIST. WE CANNOT BLAME ANYONE FOR NOT DEVELOPING OUR OWN PERSONAL RELATIONSHIP WITH GOD. ALLOW THE HOLY SPIRIT TO LEAD YOU DURING YOUR OWN PERSONAL STUDY OF THE BIBLE. DO NOT USE ANY EXSCUSES NOT TO GET TO KNOW CHRIST AND WITNESS TO

OTHERS ABOUT CHRIST. THERE IS A
PROBLEM IN THE CHURCH IF VERY
LITTLE TEACHING IS GOING ON IN
THE CHURCH, BIBLE STUDY, AND
SUNDAY SCHOOL. SOME CHRISTIANS
ARE DOING EVERYTHING EXCEPT
LEADING PEOPLE TO CHRIST. AGAIN,
WHEN I SAY LEADING PEOPLE TO
CHRIST, I ALSO MEAN THE CHRISTIAN
LIFE STYLE AS WELL. WE MUST LOOK
THE PART FIRST AND THAT'S FOR ANY
THING WE DO IN LIFE. THE BIGGEST
PROBLEM WITH MANY CHRISTIANS
IS THEY FEEL SOMEONE ELSE WILL DO
IT. OR THEY MAY FEEL IT'S THE
CHURCH OR THE PREACHER'S
RESPONSIBILTY TO WITNESS TO
OTHERS. EVERY BELIEVER IS
RESPONSIBLE FOR THEIR OWN
ACTIONS, NO ONE ELSE IS TO BLAME.
THE PROBLEM WITH MANY PEOPLE IS
THEY ALWAYS SAY THAT IT IS
SOMEONE ELSE'S FAULT, INSTEAD OF

TAKING THE REINS THEMSELVES.
STOP AND THINK FOR A MINUTE,
AND GIVE YOURSELF TIME TO
REASON WITH YOUR THOUGHTS
BEFORE MOVING ON. YOU WILL FIND
OUT; THINGS WILL WORK OUT
BETTER IN YOUR LIFE. STOP BLAMING
OTHERS FOR YOUR FAILURE IN LIFE
BECAUSE WE ARE ONLY HERE FOR A
VAPOR; TIME WILL WAIT ON NO ONE.
GET UP AND START MOVING, GET
RIGHT WITH GOD, SO YOU CAN BARE
FRUIT IN YOUR LIFE, THAT OTHERS
WILL BE ABLE TO SEE. IT IS A SHAME
WHEN OTHER CHRISTIANS, CAN'T SEE
ANY FRUIT IN YOUR LIFE. STOP
PUTTING CHRIST TO SHAME, BARE
FRUIT THAT OTHERS WILL WANT TO
TASTE AND FEEL; IT BRINGS HONESTY
TO OUR HEARTS. CHRIST IS WAITING
FOR US TO COME HOME FOR HE
CARES FOR HIS CHILDREN. BE NOT
DECEIVED **"(SIN)"** SATAN WILL KEEP

YOU AWAY FROM GOD, LONGER THAN YOU EVER WANT TO BE. LOOK TO THE **"CROSS",** THAT IS WHERE SATAN WAS DEFEATED. CHRIST PAID THE DEBT FOR US THAT WE OWED AND COULD NOT PAY OURSELVES. SO TAKE THE REINS, THEY ARE YOURS AND START LIVING AGAIN FOR CHRIST. HE (CHRIST) IS WAITING AT THE CROSS FOR YOU. REMEMBER, WE WALK ACCORDING TO HIS (GOD) **"GOSPEL."**

FOOTHOLD (CHAPTER 8)

DOES SATAN HAVE A FOOTHOLD IN YOUR LIFE?

CHRIST SHOULD BE THE CENTER OF YOUR LIFE. WE OFTEN CARRY OUR BURDENS TO ONE ANOTHER TO BE RESOLVED BY MEN OF LITTLE FAITH. I HAVE LEARNED THAT ONE IDOL WORD IS A FOOTHOLD FOR THE DEVIL, WE SHOULD BE VERY CARFUL WHO WE GET IN THE SPIRIT WITH. I KNOW YOU HAVE NEVER LOOKED AT IT THIS WAY IN THE LIGHT, SATAN IS VERY TRICKY AND CUNNING. YOU MUST BE VERY CARFUL IN CONFIDING IN THE SPIRIT WITH OTHERS BECAUSE YOU DON'T KNOW WHAT SPIRIT IS OF THEM. PEOPLE HAVE MANY SPIRITS THAT ARE EVIL AND

WILL LEAD YOU AWAY FROM GOD. THE BIBLE TELLS US TO TRY **"(TEST)"** THE SPIRIT, AND SEE IF IT IS OF ME (GOD), THERE ARE MANY SPIRITS IN THE WORLD. WE MUST PRAY WITHOUT CEASING; READING THE WORD OF GOD IN OUR DAILY LIVES. AND LOVING ONE ANOTHER AS JESUS LOVES THE CHURCH. THE CHURCH IS NOT THE BUILDING, IT IS THE PEOPLE, THAT GOD SEEKS FOR US TO LOVE. AS OUR LIGHT SHINES IN THIS EVIL AND DARK WORLD; TAKE THE GOSPEL TO EVERY ONE, BOTH SMALL AND LARGE (GREAT). IF WE WILL PRAY AND ALLOW THE HOLY SPIRIT TO GUIDE AND DIRECT OUR LIVES DAILY; WHAT AN IMPACT WE WOULD HAVE FOR JESUS CHRIST. WE CAN NO LONGER BE A PART-TIME

CHRISTIAN IN GOD'S ARMY
AND CONFESS TO KNOW JESUS
CHRIST. WE MUST ASK
OURSELVES THIS QUESTION,
ARE WE FOLLOWING CHRIST,
OR SATAN? YOU CAN NOT
SERVE BOTH MAN AND
MAMMOM **("MONEY, EARTHLY
GOODS").** SOME OF US (YOU)
HAVE BEEN PARTAKERS FOR
THE LAST TWENTY-YEARS AND
SOME LONGER. WHAT EVER
THE COST, GOD IS CALLING US
(CHRISTIANS) TO BE FULL-TIME
SERVANTS. THERE ARE TOO
MANY CHRISTIANS DRAGGING
THEIR CARS, HOUSE, BOAT,
BANK ACCOUNT, STOCK
MARKET, ETC…, TRYING TO
WITNESS FOR CHRIST. THEY
CAN'T WITNESS FOR
WORRYING ABOUT THE CARES
OF THIS WORLD, THEY ARE
CAUGHT UP IN THIS WORLD

"(SATAN'S FOOT HOLD)." YOU MUST LOOK TO THE CROSS **"(SOURCE)"** TO GUIDE YOU IN ALL TRUTH. TOO MANY PEOPLE WANT TO PLAY LIKE THEY ARE SAVED BUT HAVE NOT BEEN BORN-AGAIN. WHEN YOU HAVE BEEN BORN-AGAIN, YOUR WALK, TALK AND CONVERSATION IS DIFFERENT. YOU NO LONGER WALK WITH AN UNBELIEVING LIMP, YOU ARE A NEW CREATURE IN CHRIST. WHEN CHRISTIANS DO NOT CONFORM TO THIS WORLD, THE WORLD NO LONGER HAS ANY USE FOR US, IT SEES US AS BORING TO BE AROUND; AND THE WORLD DOESN'T WANT TO HAVE ANYTHING TO DO WITH US. REMEMBER THE WORLD LOVES THEIR OWN. IF YOU DON'T DO WHAT THEY DO, THEN YOU

ARE CONSIDERED TO BE AN
OUTCAST BY THE WORLD; BUT
NOT BY GOD. THE BIBLE TELLS
US NOT TO BE UNEQUALLY
YOKED WITH UNBELIEVERS,
FOR THEY WILL DRAW AND
GUIDE YOU AWAY FROM GOD.
WE ARE TO GUARD OUR MIND
AND HEART AT ALL TIMES,
KEEPING OUR EYES ON THE
PROMISE; THAT OUR JOY MAY
NOT BE TAKEN AWAY. GIVING
ALL THE HONOR AND GLORY
TO OUR LORD AND SAVIOR,
JESUS CHRIST. THE AUTHOR
AND FINISHER OF OUR FAITH,
WHO RENEWS OUR FAITH FROM
MORNING TO MORNING. WHO
KEEPS US SAFE AND SHIELDS
US FROM ALL HARM AND
DANGER. OUR MAIN GOAL IS
TO LOOK FOR THAT BLESSED
HOPE. WATCHING, AND
PRAYING ALWAYS. YOU HAVE

THE ANNOINTING ON YOUR
LIFE, IN WHICH JESUS CHRIST,
IS THE HEAD OF EVERY MAN.
JESUS CLEANSES OUR HEARTS
OUT, WHILE HE (JESUS) WORKS
ON OUR MIND. THE REASON HE
CLEANSES OUR HEARTS, AS
WELL AS OUR MINDS; IS SO WE
WILL NOT THINK THAT WE
WERE ALWAYS RIGHTEOUS. SO
OFTEN, WE FORGET JESUS
SAVED US FROM A PLACE OF
TORMENT **"(HELL)."** HE GAVE
US A NEW NAME AND PUT A
SONG IN OUR HEART. HE GAVE
US A NEW WALK AND A NEW
TALK. ONE DAY I SHALL HAVE
A NEW BODY **"(GLORIFIED
BODY)"** AND PRAISE THE
HEAVENLY FATHER FOR
ETERNITY. COMFORT ONE
ANOTHER, THAT WE ALL MAY
GROW AND COME TO KNOW

THE LORD; SO OUR LIVES WILL BE CHANGED AND PURIFIED.

1JOHN 3:2-3 Beloved, now are we the sons of God, and it doth not yet appear what we shall be: but we know that, when he shall appear, **we shall be like him;** for we shall see him as he is. ³ And every man that hath this hope in him **purifieth himself,** even as he is pure.

AND PLEASING IN THE SIGHT OF THE LORD (EPHESIANS 4:17-19)

MANY LIVES ARE BEING WASTED, FROM THE DECEPTION OF THE ENEMY ON PEOPLE'S MINDS. THEY ARE RECEIVING FALSE TEACHING, DEALING IN IDOLS, AND DIFFERENT KINDS OF EVIL SPIRITS. THANKS BE TO GOD, THAT WE HAVE A SAVIOR, WHO DIRECTS OUR LIVES THROUGH THE HOLY SPIRIT. LETS TAKE IT VERSE BY VERSE,

IN EPHESIANS 4:17 THEY WERE DEALING IN PRIDE, WALKING NOT IN THE WAY OF THE LORD. IT ALL STARTS IN OUR MIND, THAT'S THE REASON THE LORD TELLS US THAT OUR MIND MUST BE TRANFORMED TO BE LIKE CHRIST. WHEN WE WALK NOT IN THE SPIRIT; WE ARE SUBJECT TO DEMONS AND DIFFERENT EVIL SPIRITS. WE FAIL TO LISTEN TO THE HOLY SPIRIT, WHO GUIDES US AND LEADS US IN ALL RIGHTEOUSNESS, BUT THEIR THINKING WAS FUTILE, WHICH LED THEM DOWN A ROAD OF USELESSNESS AND IMMORAL BEHAVIOR.

VERSE 18 TO REALLY UNDERSTAND THE FUTILE OF THEIR THINKING; THINK ABOUT WHAT THE SCRIPTURES ARE SAYING, TRY WALKING

BLINDFOLDED, EVERYTHING IS DARK. THERE IS NO GOOD IN YOUR LIFE, EVERYTHING YOU TOUCH FADES AND CRUMBLE. THE PEOPLE WHO LOVE YOU, YOU BELIEVE ARE AGAINST YOU. YOUR CHILDREN DON'T WANT TO SEE YOU OR BE AROUND YOU AND PEOPLE EVEN HATE TO SEE YOU COMING. THE MAIN FOCUS IS, THERE IS NO ONE PRAYING FOR YOU. YOUR WHOLE EXSISTANCE SEEMS DARK AND YOU HAVE BECOME ALIENATED FROM GOD. THERE IS NO HAPPINESS IN THEIR LIVES, GOOD IS NOT PART OF THEIR CHARACTER AND THEIR HEARTS ARE BLINDED; BEING LED ASTRAY TO DUMB IDOLS, REACHING FOR GOALS THAT DOES NOT CONSIST OF THE SPIRIT, REACHING DOWN TO

THE BOTTOMLESS PIT, SERVING A LESSER GOD. THEY ARE UNABLE TO HEAR OR RESPOND TO GOD; PRAY THAT THEY WILL SURRENDER THEIR WILL TO CHRIST, WHO TOOK AWAY THE SINS OF THE WORLD.

VERSE 19 THEIR LUST FOR MORE AND MORE DARKENS THEIR MINDS. THEIR HEARTS ARE SO HARD, IT TAKES A CHISEL AND HAMMER TO PENETRATE THEIR HEARTS. THERE ISN'T ANY LIGHT IN THEM, THEIR HOPE IS GONE, THERE HAVE NO REMORSE OR FEELINGS, THEY DO NOT RESPECT OR CONSIDER THE FEELING'S OF OTHERS. THEY PRACTICE EVERY KIND OF IMPURITY; HIS OR HER CHARACTER IS SHAMELESS. THE BIBLE TELLS US WE MUST REPENT OF THE IMPURITY,

IMMORALITY AND SENSUALITY THAT IS IN OUR LIFE. SOME HAVE GIVEN THEMSELVES OVER TO LASCIVIOUSNESS: (GR. ASELGEIA, THAT WHICH EXCITES DISGUST)**, MEAN UNBRIDLED LUST, DEBAUCHERY, LICENTIOUS, WANTONNESS, SHAMELESSNESS, AND IT ALSO COVERS FORNICATION, AND ADULTERY.** THERE IS NO LIMIT TO THE SIN THAT HAS TAKEN HOLD OF THEM AND HAS BLINDED THEIR MINDS; TO WHERE THEY THINK ONLY WITH THEIR FLESH (FEELINGS, EMOTIONS), FOR THEY KNOW NOT THE TRUTH, THE TRUTH IS NOT IN THEIR HEARTS. SATAN HAS PUT A LIE IN THEIR HEARTS AND BLINDED THEIR MINDS FURTHER FROM THE TRUTH. THEY CAN'T SEE THE

GOOD OF THE LORD OR FEEL
THE PRESENCE OF GOD IN
THEIR LIVES. IS THE PRESENCE
OF GOD IN YOUR LIFE?

ROMANS 10:9, That if thou shalt **confess**
with thy mouth the **Lord Jesus,** and shalt
believe in thine heart that God hath **raised**
him from the **dead,** thou shalt be **saved.**

ASK TWO QUESTIONS **(1)** HAVE
YOU CONFESSED HIM AS LORD
AND SAVIOR? **(2)** DO YOU
BELIEVE THAT GOD RAISED
JESUS FROM THE DEAD, THAT
THOU SHALL BE SAVED? SO
MANY PEOPLE HAVE BELIEVED
OTHERS, FOR WHAT THEY
HAVE BEEN TOLD THEY
SHOULD BELIEVE. BUT HAVE
NOT TAKEN THE TIME TO ASK
JESUS INTO THEIR LIFE, AND
DEVELOP A PERSONAL
RELATIONSHIP WITH HIM. AS
YOU ARE READING THIS BOOK,
DO YOU KNOW OF ANYONE

WHO NEEDS JESUS IN THEIR LIFE; WHO ARE NOT ABLE TO PRAY FOR THEMSELVES? SATAN HAS TOLD THEM THAT GOD DOES NOT HEAR A SINNER'S PRAYER. **NO,** GOD DOES NOT HEAR A SINNER'S PRAYER, BUT GOD DOES HEAR A **"SINCERE PRAYER."** **"HALLELUJAH,"** IN THE NAME OF JESUS; LET US PRAY FOR THOSE WHO HAVE BEEN LED ASTRAY. WHO HAVE NO HOPE. FOR THIS DAY IS THE DAY OF SALVATION. TURNING THEIR HEARTS TO REPENTANCE. I WANT YOU TO BELIEVE ONE THING IN THE NAME OF JESUS; THE DEVIL IS **A LIE**, GOD SAID IT IN HIS WORD.

WE MUST FIRST CONFESS OUR SINS, THEN JESUS CAN AND WILL CLEANSE US FROM ALL UNRIGHTEOUSNESS. JESUS

WANTS TO PUT HIS LOVING
ARMS AROUND YOU AND HOLD
YOU. AND SAY, "MY CHILD I
WILL NEVER LEAVE YOU." YOU
HAVE BEEN BOUGHT WITH A
PRICE, FOR THE WAY HAS BEEN
PAID. THERE IS NOT ANY
DARKNESS IN HIS LOVE. LET
JESUS LEAD YOU AND WASH
YOUR SINS AWAY. THE LOVE
OF JESUS IS FROM
EVERLASTING TO
EVERLASTING. JESUS WANTS
YOU **("BELIEVER")** TO COME
HOME. YOU CAN MAKE IT TO
THE FINISH LINE, JESUS WILL
BE WAITING TO HELP YOU
FINISH. JUST TRUST HIM FOR
ALL YOUR HURTS AND
PITFALLS. JESUS IS THE WAY,
THE TRUTH, AND LIFE TO THE
FATHER. THERE IS NO PRICE,
YOU CAN PUT ON SALVATION.
MOST OF ALL, DO **NOT DOUBT**,

FIRST, YOU MUST TRUST HIM
AND AFTER YOU TRUST HIM;
YOU MUST CONFESS AND
BELIEVE (HE) **"JESUS"** IS A
FRIEND TO THE END. JESUS
WILL NEVER FORSAKE YOU OR
LEAVE YOU. LET THE SPIRIT
GUIDE YOU AND DO NOT GUIDE
YOURSELF. YOU HAVE TRIED IT
YOUR WAY AND LIFE LET YOU
DOWN; OPEN YOUR EYES THAT
YOU MAY BE ABLE TO SEE THE
GOODNESS OF THE LORD.

THE STORY OF SAUL (PAUL) ON THE ROAD TO DAMASCUS

PAUL WAS BLINDED BY THE
LIGHT THAT SHINED FROM
HEAVEN AND COULD NOT SEE
FOR THREE **DAYS;** AND HE
FASTED FOR THREE DAYS. THE
LORD SENT THE PROPHET,
ANANIAS, TO LAY HANDS ON
SAUL (PAUL), WHO REGAINED
HIS SIGHT, AND WAS FILLED

WITH THE HOLY GHOST
(SPIRIT). NOTHING IS TO HARD
FOR GOD; BUT WE MUST
BELIEVE, TRUST AND OBEY
HIM. HE (JESUS) WILL OPEN UP
THE WINDOWS OF HEAVEN,
GOD IS SO WONDERFUL. HIS
WORD IS FROM EVERLASTING
TO EVERLASTING. LET'S PRAY
THAT EVERY NATION WILL
RECEIVE THE TRUTH; AND
PRAY FOR EVERYONE YOU
KNOW TO RECEIVE THE TRUTH,
THAT THEIR SINS WILL BE
FORGIVEN IN THE NAME OF
THE FATHER, SON, AND HOLY
GHOST (SPIRIT). THEY WERE
TAUGHT TO PUT OFF THE OLD
MAN AND PUT ON THE NEW
MAN. IF WE ARE GOING TO LIVE
THE LIFE OF CHRIST, THE FLESH
MUST BE "**CRUCIFIED.**"

JUSTIFICATION (CHAPTER 9)

JUSTIFICATION: WHERE THE SINNER WAS DECLARED **"GUILTY",** AND IS NOW IS DECLARED **"INNOCENT",** SET APART, AND FOUND NOT GUILTY ON THE BASIS OF WHAT CHRIST DID ON THE **"CROSS".** MAN IS GUILTY FOR WHAT ADAM DID, ONLY IN CHRIST CAN MAN BE **"PARDONED",** HIS SINS ARE FORGIVEN HIM, HE IS NOW A SON AND NOT A BASTARD. ADAM SINNED IN THE GARDEN THAT PAVED THE WAY FOR EVERY MAN. THIS IS THE REASON MAN CAN'T SAVE HIMSELF, NO MATTER HOW HARD HE TRIES TO LIVE WITHOUT THE BLOOD; MAN IS STILL**"GUILTY."** HOW CAN THIS

BE TRUE WHEN I HAVE NOT
COMMITTED ANY OF THE SINS
YOU SAY I HAVE COMMITTED?
FOR EXAMPLE, IF YOU HAVE
NEVER HAD A DRINK A DAY IN
YOUR LIFE, REGARDLESS OF
THE FACT, WE ARE STILL
"GUILTY." IT WAS HARD FOR
ME TO UNDERSTAND AT FIRST;
UNTIL GOD SHOWED ME IN HIS
(GOD) **"WORD",** WE MUST LOOK
TO GOD IF WE ARE TO
UNDERSTAND HIS (GOD'S)
WORD.

JAMES 1:5, If any of you lack **wisdom,**
let him ask of God, that giveth to all *men*
liberally, and upbraideth not; **and it shall be
given him.**

NONE OF US IS RIGHTEOUS.
WHAT JESUS DID FOR US ON
THE CROSS, MADE IT ALL
POSIBLE FOR OUR SALVATION;
AND NOT BY OUR OWN WORKS
OF RIGHTEOUSNESS.

TITUS 3:5-7 Not by works of righteousness which we have done, but according to his mercy he saved us, **by the washing of regeneration, and renewing of the Holy Ghost;** 6 Which he shed on us abundantly **through Jesus Christ our Saviour;** 7 That being justified by his grace, we should be made heirs according to the hope of eternal life.

VERSE 5 THIS IS IMPOSSIBLE WITH MAN, ONLY THE HOLY GHOST (SPIRIT) CAN MAKE THIS POSSIBLE FOR MAN TO BE SAVED. EVEN WHEN MAN GETS SAVED, HIS WORKS STILL DOES NOT SAVE HIM. ONLY WHAT HE DOES FOR THE LORD AND MAN LOOKING TO THE CROSS; THEN, ONLY IS GOD PLEASED, BY HIS FAITH IN CHRIST.

VERSE 6 ABUNDANTLY: MEANS **"PLENTY",** HIS (JESUS) LOVE FOR US IS AGAPE, **UNCONDITIONAL:** IT IS COMMITTED AND CHOSEN LOVE THAT DOESN'T HAVE

ANY FEAR OR BLEMISH. IT'S HIS (JESUS) MERCY AND GRACE THAT KEEPS US, GIVES US THAT SECOND CHANCE; TIME AND TIME AGAIN.

VERSE 7, BEEN JUSTIFIED BY HIS GRACE WE HAVE ALL THAT THE CROSS HAS FOR US WHO HAS BEEN BORN-AGAIN.

READ ROMANS 5:1-21 LAY IT ALL OUT VERY CLEARLY

HOW THE JUSTIFICATION PROCESS WORK, FIRST WE ARE

WASHED: JESUS CLEANSED US FROM OUR SINS AND WASHED US WITH HIS LOVE FROM THIS WORLD LUST, SIN, ETC..., THIS IS AN ON GOING **"SANTIFICATION PROCESS"** FOR THE BELIEVER; IT STARTED FROM THE DAY OF CONVERSION TO THE DAY

CHRIST CALLS US HOME TO BE WITH HIM (JESUS) FOREVER AND FOREVER. WE MUST GUARD OUR MIND, HEART AND SOUL; THAT WE DON'T COME UNTO COMDEMNATION.

SANCTIFIED: IT IS NOT PERFECTION, THE HOLY SPIRIT DIRECTS OUR PATH AND KEEPS US ON THE NARROW; BRINGING US TO A SAVING GRACE, KEPING US PURE AND MAKING US CLEAN. WE ARE SET APART BY THE HOLY SPIRIT. THIS IS DEALING WITH TRUTH. WE NO LONGER HAVE FELLOWSHIP WITH THE WORLD AND THE LUST OF THE WORLD. WE WALK DAILY WITH CHRIST OUR LORD, WHO IS THE PROPITIATION FOR OUR SINS, WHO CANCELS OUT OUR DEBT.

JUSTIFIED: WE ARE PARDONED AND DECLARED NOT GUILTY.

WE NO LONGER OWE THE DEBT
BECAUSE JESUS PAID IT FOR
THE WORLD ON THE CROSS.
EVERYONE CAN BE SAVED
WHO WANTS TO BE SAVED;
REGARDLESS OF THE COLOR OF
YOUR SKIN OR RELIGION.
CHRIST PAID IT ALL IN FULL.
GOD IS WELL PLEASED WITH
HIS SON JESUS CHRIST, THE
CROSS MADE IT ALL POSSIBLE
FOR BELIEVERS. EVERYTHING
IS IN THE NAME OF THE LORD
JESUS AND BY THE SPIRIT OF
GOD.

ARE YOU LIVING BY BREAD ALONE (CHAPTER 10)

MATTHEW 4:4 But he answered and said, It is written, Man shall not live by bread alone, **but by every word that proceedeth out of the mouth of God.**

DOES MAN (YOU) LIVE BY EVERY WORD?

THE FIRST THING I WANT YOU TO DO IS TO PRAY AND ASK GOD WHERE DO YOU STAND WITH HIM, PLEASE DON'T TAKE THIS FOR GRANTED, IT MAY BE THE LAST TIME FOR YOU TO REPENT OF ALL YOUR SINS, I WAS ONCE LIVING BY BREAD ALONE, LET ME EXPLAIN TO YOU WHAT GOD MEANT IN HIS (GOD) WORD. THERE WERE THINGS IN THE BIBLE I DID NOT AGREE WITH GOD ON, I'M JUST

BEING REAL, THE PROBLEM
WITH ME (MAN) WAS THERE
WERE WAYS THAT SEEMED
RIGHT TO ME, BUT IN THE EYES
OF THE LORD, THEY ARE
WRONG. LET ME BE CLEAR, I
WAS SAVED, MANY MEN ARE
SAVED, BUT THEY ARE LIVING
BY BREAD ALONE; THIS IS A
"SANTIFICATION PROCESS."
GOD'S GRACE AND MERCY IS
WHAT KEEPS US IN HIS LOVE,
BUT DON'T TAKE HIS LOVE FOR
GRANTED, GOD **"FORBID"**
THERE ARE MANY MEN TODAY
THAT ARE LIVING BY BREAD
ALONE AND DON'T KNOW IT.
THEY CONFESS TO BE SAVED,
BUT ARE LIVING IN SIN AND
HAVE NOT **"REPENTED."** THEY
GO TO CHURCH, SOME SING IN
THE CHOIR, SERVE ON THE
DEACON BOARD AND EVEN
PREACH. PEOPLE THINK

BECAUSE THEY GO TO CHURCH THAT THEY ARE ALRIGHT IF THEY BELONG TO A CERTAIN DENOMINATION. TO BE SAVED IS TO BE **"BORN-AGAIN",** AND NOT TO THE THINGS OF THIS WORLD. OR BY GIVING THE PREACHER YOUR HAND; NOR BECAUSE MY GRANNY WAS A MEMBER OF THE CHURCH. YOU MUST HAVE A PERSONAL RELATIONSHIP WITH THE LORD. NO ONE CAN STAND FOR YOU, THERE ISN'T ANY USE IN SAYING, "ASK THE PREACHER." HE CAN'T HELP YOU, ONLY THE RELATONSHIP WITH JESUS CHRIST WILL GET YOU A TICKET IN THE KINGDOM. **"RELIGION"** IS ONE OF THE MOST POWERFUL WEAPONS SATAN USES TO CONTROL THE APOSTATE CHURCH. BUT THE SEVEN CHURCHES IN THE BOOK

OF REVELATION WAS HERE FOR
MAN TO SEE HIS WAYS, AND TO
AMEND HIS WAYS. IN OTHER
WORDS; THEY WERE PUT HERE
FOR MAN TO FOLLOW AND
THAT IS GOD'S WORD. MANY
SHALL TAKE THE ROAD TO
DESTRUCTION BECAUSE THEY
ARE LIVING BY BREAD ALONE.
BE NOT DECEIVED, SATAN HAS
NO NEUTRAL GROUND. THERE
ARE ONLY TWO ROADS, AND
THAT IS THE **STRAIT AND
NARROW**. THE **STRAIT** IS
"DESTRUCTION" THAT LEDS
TO HELL; THIS IS REAL. MOST
PEOPLE THINK WHEN THEY DIE
THAT'S IT, DON'T LET THIS LIE
KEEP YOU FROM THE TRUTH.
MANY MEN (MAN OR WOMAN)
WILL GO DOWN THIS ROAD OF
NO RETURN AND WILL BE
SEPARATED FROM GOD FOR
ETERNITY. NO ONE WILL BE

ABLE TO HELP YOU. YOU WILL
BE TORMENTED IN **HELL** AND
AFTER THE 1000 YEARS IS UP IN
THE **MILLENNIUM**, THEN YOU
WILL STAND AT THE GREAT
WHITE THRONE. AND IF YOU
ARE NOT FOUND WRITTEN IN
THE BOOK OF LIFE, YOU WILL
BE CAST IN THE **LAKE OF FIRE**;
WHERE SATAN, ALL THE
ANGELS THAT FOLLOWED
SATAN, THE ANTI-CHRIST AND
THE FALSE PROPHET WILL BE
IN THE LAKE OF FIRE FOREVER
AND FOREVER. IF YOU ARE
READING THIS AND YOU ARE
NOT SAVED OR YOU DON'T
KNOW HIM (JESUS), IN THE
PARDON OF YOUR SINS, ASK
JESUS TO COME IN YOUR
HEART AND ASK FOR
FORGIVENESS. HE (GOD) WILL
SEND HIS (SON) TO LIVE IN
YOUR HEART WITH YOU FOR

EVER AND EVER IF YOU ARE BORN-AGAIN, MEANING **"PURE IN SPIRIT",** LET'S TALK ABOUT THE **NARROW** IS LIFE AND THAT LIFE IS **ONLY IN JESUS** AND NO OTHER.

THERE WILL BE ONLY A FEW THAT WILL FIND THEIR WAY, YOU MUST TRUST HIM AND BELIEVE WITH ALL YOUR HEART; DOUBTING, AND WAVING NOTHING. **"LISTEN TO NO ONE"**, BUT THE WORDS OF GOD. MEN WILL TRY TO TELL YOU THAT YOU ARE ALRIGHT. SOME PREACHERS WILL SAY, LET ME SHOW YOU THE WAY; RUN FROM THEM. WHAT I MEAN IS KEEP YOUR EYES ON THE WORD **("CROSS")** OF GOD. PUT NO TRUST IN **NO MAN**, BECAUSE MAN WILL FAIL YOU, HE HAS NO HELL OR HEAVEN TO PUT YOU IN, HE IS GOING TO

BE JUDGED AS WELL. WE NEED
EVERY WORD OF GOD, IF WE
ARE GOING TO FOLLOW JESUS.
WITHOUT EVERY WORD, GOD
CAN'T ACCEPT YOUR
OFFERING, CAIN TRIED IT AND
FAILED. **"BREAD"** IS NOTHING
BUT **"DESTRUCTION."** BE NOT
DECEIVED, FOR SATAN HAS
BUT A SHORT TIME TO DECEIVE
AS MANY FOLLOWERS AS HE
(SATAN) CAN. KEEP YOUR EYES
ON THE CROSS, FOR THE CROSS
WILL BRING FRUIT IN YOUR
LIFE. GET ALL THAT
BITTERNESS OUT OF YOUR
HEART, AND MAKE YOU A NEW
CREATURE IN CHRIST.   GOD
SENT HIS SON IN THE WORLD
TO REDEEM MAN, SO THAT
MAN WOULD BE FREE FROM
THE BONDAGE OF THIS WORLD;
WHICH SATAN HAS A HOLD ON.
DO NOT BE DECEIVED OF

SATAN'S DEVICES. THEY ARE
ONLY A TRICK TO GET YOU TO
SERVE HIM (SATAN), AND HIS
KINGDOM. FOR THE DAYS ARE
NO MORE THAN A VAPOR, SEEK
GOD WHILE GOD IS TO BE
FOUND. TIME HAS RAN OUT ON
SO MANY PEOPLE BECAUSE
THEY THOUGHT THEY HAD
TIME TO GET IT TOGETHER;
THAT'S THE MISTAKE SATAN
WANTS YOU TO ACCEPT SO
THAT HE (SATAN) CAN FILL
YOUR MIND WITH TIME, THAT
YOU DON'T HAVE IN THIS
WORLD. SATAN WILL DO ALL
AND ANYTHING TO KEEP YOU
AWAY FROM THE CROSS
BECAUSE SATAN KNOWS THAT
YOU WILL HAVE PROTECTION;
AND HE (SATAN) WILL HAVE
NO MORE POWER OVER YOU.
GOD WILL PUT HIS SPIRIT IN
YOU. YOUR EYES AND EARS

WILL OPEN UP TO SEE GOD'S
LIGHT, THAT SHINES BRIGHT IN
THE LIFE OF THE BELEIVER
WHO CAN HEAR HIS VOICE.
SATAN CAN'T STOP YOU, ONLY
YOU CAN ALLOW YOURSELF TO
BE BLINDED BY THE FALSE
LIGHT, THAT SATAN HAS
BLINDED SO MANY PEOPLE
AND HAVE LED THEM ASTRAY
TO NO RETURN. LISTEN TO THE
WORDS OF GOD. "**EVERY
WORD THAT PROCEEDETH
OUT OF THE MOUTH OF GOD**",
THAT IS WHAT IS GOING TO
SAVE YOU; AND THE ONLY
THING THAT WILL SAVE YOU
FROM THIS **"EVIL, AND
ADULTEROUS WORLD."** STOP
LOOKING BACK, IT ONLY KEEPS
YOU FROM HEARING THE
WORDS OF GOD, WE MUST
CONFESS OUR SINS BEFORE
GOD. THE FIRST THING IS, YOU

MUST HEAR SOMETHING FIRST,
AND THAT IS THE WORD OF
GOD. THE WORD MUST BE REAL
IN YOUR LIFE, BEFORE SATAN
CAN START THE PROCESS OF
GETTING YOU BACK ON HIS
SIDE. SO MANY CHRISTIANS
HAVE GONE BACK IN THE
WORLD. BECAUSE THEY FAIL
TO HEAR, AND BELIEVE EVERY
WORD THAT PROCEEDETH OUT
OF THE MOUTH OF GOD. JESUS
IS YOUR ONLY HOPE FOR
TODAY AND TOMORROW. DO
NOT LET THE **"BREATH"**
(SPIRIT) BE TAKEN AWAY FROM
YOU. GET THE SPIRIT OF
CHRIST, SO THAT YOU CAN
LIVE FOR ETERNITY WITH
CHRIST. AND THAT IS TO GIVE
YOUR HEART TO CHRIST, SO
THAT YOU CAN BE SAVED
FROM THE DARKNESS OF THIS
WORLD.

TITHING (CHAPTER 11)

TITHE: TO GIVE A TENTH OF
YOUR EARNINGS TO THE
CHURCH, FOR THE FURTHERING
OF THE GOSPEL. FIRST OF ALL,
LET'S GET AN UNDERSTANDING
OF THE CHURCH. GOD DOES
NOT NEED YOUR MONEY, HE
(GOD) OWNS THE CATTLE ON
THE HILL; EVERYTHING BE
LONGS TO GOD. WE ARE JUST
BORROWING WHAT IS GOD'S IN
THE FIRST PLACE. WE ARE NOT
SUPPOSE TO BE GIVING TO A
BUILDING. WHAT I MEAN IS
MAN IS NOT TO TAKE THE
MONEY BECAUSE HE FEELS
THAT IT BELONGS TO HIM
(PREACHER, JANITOR,
YARDMAN, MUSICIAN, ETC…,
THE BIBLE STATES THAT A
MAN IS WORTH HIS HIRE,
MEANING IF HE OR SHE WORKS;

THEY ARE TO BE PAID, BUT
THIS DOES NOT APPLY TO
EVERY ONE IN THE MINISTRY,
WHEN YOU TITHE, DO NOT
SOUND THE ALARM; MEANING
DO NOT LET YOUR RIGHT HAND
KNOW WHAT YOUR LEFT HAND
IS DOING. I HAVE FOUND THAT
WHEN A MAN OR WOMAN IS
BLESSED THEY DON'T HAVE TO
STEAL FROM GOD, OR THE
CHURCH. "(**PEOPLE**)" IN OTHER
WORDS, THEY DON'T HAVE TO
COVET, OR THINK THE CHURCH
OWES THEM SOMETHING;
WHEN EVERY ONE HAS GIFT(S)
AND TALENT(S). WHETHER A
PERSON IS PAID, DEPENDS ON
THE SITUATION. FOR EXAMPLE,
IF YOU ARE CALLED TO THE
MINISTRY FULL TIME **"YES"**
BUT PART TIME **"NO."** BUT IF
THE CHURCH AGREES TO THIS,
THE MINISTER SHOULD BE

ABLE TO FULFILL A FULL TIME
DUTY IN THE CHURCH, WHICH
IS IMPOSIBLE, IF THEY ARE
WORKING A JOB. I'M JUST
BEING HONEST AND STRAIGHT.
I DON'T SEE ANYTHING WRONG
WITH PASTOR'S APPRECIATION
DAY, IF THEY ARE NOT
DRAWING A SALARY; THIS IS
MY UNDERSTANDING FROM
THE WORD OF GOD. IN THE OLD
TESTAMENT, THE PEOPLE GAVE
TO THE LEVI, AND THE TENTH
OF WHAT THEY HAD WENT TO
THE PRIESTS FOR THEM TO
LIVE ON. THIS WAS GOD'S
WORD AND NOT MAN'S
DECISION. WE HAVE FEW
CHRISTIANS TODAY TO MAKE
THE RIGHT DECISIONS; AND
NINETY-NINE PERCENT WON'T
PREACH OR DO ANYTHING IN
THE CHURCH UNLESS THEY
ARE PAID, THIS IS THE

"LAODICEA CHURCH." WE SHOULD ALL GIVE OUR TIME, TALENT AND MONEY TO THE CHURCH FOR WE ALL ARE ONE BODY IN CHRIST. ONE PART CAN'T DO ANYTHING WITHOUT THE OTHER PART OF THE BODY, THAT IS THE REASON THE CHURCH CAN'T GROW IS BECAUSE THE CHURCH IS NOT ON ONE ACCORD. GOD IS NOT GOING TO BLESS NO MESS. GOD IS NOT OF CONFUSION, GOD WANTS EVERYTHING IN ORDER AND THAT IS THE WAY GOD INTENTED FOR IT TO BE; THIS IS WHAT PLEASES GOD.

WILL A MAN ROB GOD (MALACHI 3:8-12)

VERSE 8 "YES", THE PRIESTS WERE BRINGING THE SICK AND THE LAME ANIMALS TO THE ALTAR FOR SACRIFICE, AND WERE POLLUTING THE ALTAR,

IN "**THE DISPOSATION PERIOD OF GRACE**" WE HAVE A DIFFERENT SYSTEM TODAY, IT IS CALLED FURTHERING THE GOSPEL. WE STILL GIVE TO THE LORD, BUT IN A DIFFERENT WAY, THIS IS CALLED BEING A CHEERFUL GIVER. IN THE OLD TESTAMENT, MAN WAS "**COMMANDED**" TO GIVE "**TEN PERCENT**" BACK TO THE LORD, WE STILL GIVE TEN PERCENT TODAY. I'LL MAKE AN "**ANALOGY**" (COMPARISON): IF A FARMER PLANTS THREE ROWS OF CORN, THE "**FIRST ROW**" IS FOR HIM AND HIS FAMILY, THE "**SECOND ROW**" IS TO GIVE BACK TO THE CHURCH; AND THE "**THRID ROW**" IS TO HELP THY NEIGHBOR, AND THAT IS GIVING BACK TO THE LORD. REMEMBER THE LORD DOES

NOT NEED OUR MONEY, THE LORD OWNS THE HILLS AND THE CATTLE. EVERYTHING BELONGS TO THE LORD. WE ARE JUST BORROWING FROM THE LORD, WHAT IS ALREADY THE LORD'S. ABRAHAM PAID TITHES TO **"MELCHIZEDEK A TYPE OF CHRIST",** THIS WAS THE FIRST OF THE BEGINNING OF THE TITHING. GOD CALLED ABRAHAM OUT OF HIS COUNTRY TO BE A GREAT NATION, AND ALL FAMILIES SHALL BE BLESSED IN THEE (ABRAHAM). EVERYONE THAT BELIEVES IN THE NAME OF CHRIST, MUST BE A TITHER: **"A CHEERFUL GIVER."** THE CURSE MUST BE LIFTED OFF OF YOU, IF YOU ARE GOING TO BE BLESSED IN THE NAME OF JESUS, YOU MUST REPENT OF THAT **"SIN"** FOR NO SIN SHALL

ENTER IN THE KINGDOM OF
HEAVEN.

VERSE 9 WE CAN'T **"ROB"** GOD,
AND STILL BE BLESSED. THE
PRIEST HAD TO LEARN THAT
LESSON, WHICH THEY NEVER
DID. UNTIL YOU LEARN AND
REPENT OF YOUR SINS, YOU
WILL BE UNDER A **"CURSE"**
ALL THE DAYS OF YOUR LIFE.
YOU WILL NEVER ENJOY THE
FRUIT THAT THE LORD HAS FOR
YOU. YOUR FRUIT WILL
ALLWAYS BE ROTTEN AND
SPOILED BECAUSE MAN
REFUSES TO OBEY THE WORD
OF GOD; AND LIVE A LIFE OF
PEACE, JOY, AND HAPPINESS.
WITHOUT THE LORD, THERE IS
NO PEACE. WHEN A MAN IS
UNDER A **"CURSE"** HIS
BLESSINGS ARE CUT OFF.
EVERYTHING HE TOUCHES
FAILS, THE MORE HE RECEIVES

THE LESS HE HAS AND GIVES; BECAUSE MAN DOES NOT HAVE ANYTHING WITHOUT THE LORD. FOR THE LORD IS OUR "**ROCK**", AND OUR "**SHIELD.**" THE LORD IS A SHIELD TO THEM WHO PUT THEIR TRUST IN HIM (**LORD**). LET THE LORD LIFT THE "**CURSE**" TODAY, ONLY IN THE LORD IS PEACE MY BROTHER, AND SISTER.

VERSE 1O THE LORD IS ASKING US TO "**PROVE**" HIM, THE LORD WANTS TO LIFT THE "**CURSE**" FROM YOU; THAT SATAN WILL NOT SPOIL THE FRUIT OF YOUR LAND, YOU ARE UNDER A "**CURSE**" AS LONG AS YOU "**ROB**" GOD OF HIS (LORD) TITHES. THE PRIESTS WERE TO BRING MEAT IN THE STOREHOUSE, BUT INSTEAD THEY STOLE FROM THE LORD; BY BRINGING THE LAME AND

THE SICK. PEOPLE DO THAT
TODAY AS WELL, THEY GIVE
WHAT THEY DON'T WANT ,
AND KEEP THE GOOD FOR
THEMSELVES. THIS IS "**GREED**";
YOU WILL NEVER BE ABLE TO
BREAK THE **"CURSE"** BY
GIVING LESS THAN WHAT IS
GOD'S, IN THE FIRST PLACE. IF
YOU CAN'T LIVE OUT OF THE
NINETY PERCENT, HOW WILL
YOU BE ABLE TO LIVE WITHN
THE HUNDRED PERCENT?
THAT'S THE REASON SATAN
DOES NOT WANT YOU TO
TITHE, BECAUSE SATAN WANTS
TO KEEP YOU UNDER A
"CURSE." NEVER ALLOWING
ANY GOOD FRUIT IN YOUR
LIFE. THE LORD WILL CAST
THAT TREE IN THE FIRE, FOR IT
IS **"CORRUPT."** FOR IT CAN'T
BRING ANYTHING BUT BAD
FRUIT.

VERSE 11 THE LORD WILL PLANT YOUR TREE BY A RIVER, THAT IT MAY BRING FORTH GOOD FRUIT. GOD WILL NOT ALLOW SATAN TO **"DEVOUR"** YOUR FRUIT, THERE SHALL BE PLENTY IN YOUR VINEYARD, RUNING OVER, AND LACKING NOTHING. WHEN THE GLASS GET'S LOW, THE LORD WILL FILL IT BACK UP AGAIN; THAT IS THE WAY IT WILL BE. PLENTY FRUIT ON THE TREE, THAT YOU WILL LEARN TO SHARE WITH OTHERS; THAT IS WHAT IT MEANS TO BE A CHEERFUL GIVER. REMEMBER, I SAID THAT THE LORD DID NOT NEED OUR MONEY? THE LORD OWNS THE HILLS AND THE CATTLE. PEOPLE WILL CALL YOU **"BLESSED"**, YOU WILL HAVE AN **"OVER FLOW"** IN THE LORD. REMEMBER, SATAN'S

JOB IS TO KEEP YOU UNDER A "**CURSE**" AND KEEP YOU FROM ENJOYING WHAT GOD HAS FOR YOU. IF SATAN CAN STEAL YOUR JOY, HE CAN KEEP WHAT EVER IS "**YOURS.**" GOD WANTS TO BREAK THAT **"CURSE"** SO THAT YOU CAN LIVE IN PEACE, AND ENJOY THE BLESSINGS THE LORD HAS FOR YOU. SATAN DOES NOT HAVE TO BE IN CONTROL OF YOUR LIFE; GOD WANTS TO BE IN CONTROL OF YOUR LIFE.

VERSE 12 YOU SHALL BE BLESSED IN WHAT EVER YOUR HAND TOUCHES. THE REASON SO MANY CHRISTIANS ARE NOT BLESSED IS BECAUSE THEY REFUSE TO TRUST GOD, AND THEY ARE NOT OBEDIENT. THEY CAN'T LET GO OF WHAT THEY THINK THEY HAVE, THAT THEY DON'T HAVE. YOU WILL

FIND OUT THAT IT'S SO
PLEASING IN THE LORD, TO
WALK IN THE LORD'S WAYS; I
HAVE BEEN A TITHER FOR
ABOUT THIRTY-NINE OR
FORTY-YEARS, THE LORD'S
WORD IS TRUE, THE LORD WILL
OPEN THE WINDOWS OF
HEAVEN, **"BLESSINGS WILL
FLOW",** THE LORD TAKES CARE
OF ALL MY NEEDS, I DON'T
HAVE TO WORRY ABOUT
NOTHING. JUST BE OBEDIENT
TO THE LORD'S WILL, FOR HE
LOVES US AND WILL TAKE
CARE OF HIS CHILDREN. YOU
SHALL BE **"BLESSED"** IN WHAT
EVER YOU DO, SO FOLLOW THE
SPIRIT, IT WILL NOT LEAD YOU
DOWN THE WRONG PATH. IT
WILL LIVE WITH YOU DAY AND
NIGHT; IT WILL BE SWEET
SLEEP TO YOU. **"THE LORD
LOVES A CHEERFUL GIVER",**

AND BY HIS BLOOD WE HAVE
"REDEMPTION" AND WE HAVE
ALL WE NEED IN THE CROSS.

THE RAPTURE OF THE CHURCH (CHAPTER 12)

WHEN WILL THE RAPTURE TAKE PLACE? MAN DOES NOT KNOW, ONLY GOD, WE ARE TO WATCH, AND PRAY

THE ANGELS IN HEAVEN DON'T KNOW, NOR THE SON, AND NO MAN; BUT ONLY GOD. IN THAT DAY, **"GOD"** WILL MAKE THAT DECISION, AND NO ONE ELSE. GOD HAS CREATED, THE WRATH THAT WILL FALL ON MAN IN THAT DAY, FOR GOD WILL DESTROY ALL UNRIGHTEOUS PEOPLE WHOSE NAME IS NOT WRITTEN IN THE BOOK OF LIFE. FOR GOD GAVE MAN PLENTY OF TIME AND ROOM TO REPENT OF HIS AND HER SINS. SOME WILL EVEN HIDE THEMSELVES UNDER AND AROUND THE ROCKS, TO TRY

TO ESCAPE GOD'S **"WRATH."**
WE MUST PRAY AND WATCH
FOR WE KNOW NOT THE HOUR
NOR THE DAY WHEN THE LORD
WILL RETURN. MAN HAS
REJECTED THE WORD OF GOD
TO A POINT OF NO RETURN.
MEANING MAN'S HEART IS
EVIL, HE WILL NOT LOOK TO
GOD FOR **"REDEMPTION"** IN
THE CROSS, THAT HE MAY BE
SAVED. THEIR WILL BE FEW
THAT WILL BE WATCHING FOR
THE LORD TO RETURN FOR HIS
CHURCH, REMEMBER THIS IS
THE **"LAODICEA CHURCH"**
(APOSTATE), PEOPLE THAT
PRETEND TO BE SAVED TODAY.
THEY WILL BE DOING
EVERYTHING, BUT WAITING
FOR THE LORD, THIS IS
HAPPENING THIS DAY AND
TIME. PEOPLE ARE MORE
CONCERNED ABOUT THE

THINGS OF THIS WORLD, THAN
THE THINGS OF GOD. FIRST OF
ALL MANY PEOPLE ARE NOT
SAVED, THEY HAVE A FORM OF
GODLINESS AND NO POWER.
THEY HAVE PUT THEIR TRUST
IN THE WRONG THING, THEIR
EARS ARE DULL OF HEARING
AND THEY CAN'T EVEN SEE
BECAUSE THEIR EYES ARE DIM.
YOU HAVE THE BLIND LEADING
THE BLIND AND THEY ALL ARE
GOING TO FALL IN THE DITCH
BECAUSE THEY REFUSE TO
LISTEN TO THE WORD OF GOD
AND BE SAVED. YOU MUST
HEAR SOMETHING FIRST AND
THAT IS THE WORD OF GOD;
TOO MANY PEOPLE ARE LIVING
BY BREAD ALONE, MANY ARE
SERVING TWO MASTERS. SOME
DESPISING THE OTHER AND
SOME HOLDING TO THE OTHER.
WE MUST BE OF ONE SPIRIT IN

CHRIST IF WE ARE TO LIVE
WITH HIM FOR ETERNITY.
MANY PEOPLE WILL BE SLEEP;
THEY WILL NOT HAVE AN EAR
TO HEAR THE TRUMPET SOUND
BECAUSE THEY ONLY HAVE A
FORM OF GODLINESS AND NO
POWER. THEY DID NOT
"CRUCIFY THE FLESH",
ALLOWING JESUS TO BE LORD
OF THEIR LIVES; THEY KEPT
DOING THE THINGS THAT WERE
NOT PLEASING TO GOD, AND
HAVE NOT THE SPIRIT OF
CHRIST TO ENTER THE
KINGDOM OF GOD. EACH MAN
MUST WATCH FOR HIMSELF.
YOU WILL NOT BE ABLE, ON
THAT DAY, WHEN THE
RAPTURE COMES; TO WAKE UP
ANYONE ELSE OR GO AND FIND
SOMEONE ELSE. THEY WILL BE
LEFT BEHIND. THE MOVIE LEFT
BEHIND IS A TRUE MOVIE;

MANY WILL CRY IN THAT DAY
TO BE **"RAPTURED",** EVEN
LIVING IN ANXIETY. GOD IS
LOOKING FOR A CHURCH
WITHOUT SPOT OR WRINKLE,
ONLY THE **"PURE IN SPIRIT"**
WILL SEE GOD, **("THAT IS BE
WITH GOD FOR ETERNITY").**
BE NOT DECEIVED BY THE
TRICKERY OF SATAN AND HIS
DEVICES; FOR MANY ARE
FOLLOWING THE FABLES AND
BELIEVING; ADDING AND
TAKING AWAY FROM THE
WORD OF GOD. THERE ARE
MANY DIFFERENT DOCTRINES
IN THE CHURCH TODAY AND
MAN IS NOT LED BY THE SPIRIT
OF GOD. SO MANY ARE LED BY
SEDUCING SPIRITS, THEIR
FAITH IS IN EVERYTHING
EXCEPT THE WORD OF GOD;
THEIR IDOLS ARE ALL THEY
WANT TO PLAY WITH. THE

WORD OF GOD IS ON THE BACK
BURNER. THERE SHALL BE
WEEPING AND GNASHING OF
TEETH IN THESE LAST DAYS,
WE ARE LIVING IN. I ALSO
BELIEVE WE ARE IN PERILOUS
TIMES, PEOPLE DON'T CARE
ABOUT ONE ANOTHER ANY
MORE. THEY CARE ONLY
ABOUT THEMSELVES; **IT'S ME,
MYSELF, AND I**. KEEP
"WATCHING" AND **"PRAYING"**,
THE LORD WILL SET THINGS IN
ORDER WHEN HE (JESUS)
COMES THE SECOND TIME
WITH HIS SAINTS TO MEET THE
SAINTS IN THE AIR.

**WHO WILL GO IN THE
RAPTURE? FIRST OFALL THE
RAPTURE CAN TAKE PLACE
AT ANY TIME**

ONLY THE **PURE IN HEART**
WILL SEE JESUS AND REIN
WITH JESUS FOR ETERNITY,

THERE WILL ONLY BE A **"FEW"**, WHO WILL GO IN THE RAPTURE AN HAVE A **"GLORIFIED BODY",** THE REST WILL BE LEFT BEHIND, WE WILL NOT KNOW WHEN THE TRIBULATION WILL START, BUT WE DO KNOW WHEN THE **"TREATY IS SIGNED"** THE **"TRIBULATION"** WILL BEGIN AND LAST FOR SEVEN YEARS, THEN PRIOR TO THE SEVEN YEARS ENDING, OR AT THE END OF THE SEVEN YEARS; CHRIST WILL RETURN WITH HIS SAINTS AND ANGELS, WHICH IS THE SECOND COMING OF CHRIST.

1THESSALONIANS 4:13-18, WHO WILL GET A NEW BODY?

VERSE 13

THE DEAD IN CHRIST, FROM ADAM TO CHRIST COMING TO

MEET THE SAINTS IN THE AIR
TO GIVE THE SAINTS A PERFECT
BODY "**(GLORIFIED BODIES)**",
THEM WHICH ARE ASLEEP,
REFERS TO **BELEIVERS**, THE
OTHERS ARE **DEAD**, ONLY THE
CHURCH WILL GO IN THE
RAPTURE TO BE WITH THE
LORD FOREVER AND EVER; THE
SAD THING IS MANY PEOPLE
BELIEVE THEY HAVE A TICKET
TO HEAVEN, WHEN SATAN HAS
STOLEN THEIR TICKET TO
ENTER IN HEAVEN TO BE WITH
GOD FOR ALL ETERNITY.
WHAT WILL KEEP YOU FROM
ENTERING THE KINGDOM?
**"THE REJECTING OF JESUS
(THE CROSS) AND A PERSON
LOOSING HIS OR HER FAITH".**

VERSE. 14

JESUS DIED AND ROSE AGAIN;
GOD RAISED JESUS FROM THE
GRAVE, AND THOSE WHICH

"SLEEP IN JESUS", THESE ARE ALREADY IN HEAVEN WITH JESUS WAITING FOR THAT DAY WHEN THE **"LAST TRUMPET"** WILL BLOW. THE RAPTURE OF THE CHURCH OR THE RESURRECTION OF ALL BELIEVERS TO MEET THE LORD IN THE AIR.

1CORINTHIANS 15: 51-52

[51] Behold, I shew you a **mystery;** We shall not all sleep, but we shall all be changed,
[52] In a moment, in the twinkling of an eye, at the **last trump:** for the trumpet shall sound, and the dead shall be **raised incorruptible,** and we shall be changed.

VERSE. 15

PREVENT THEM WHICH ARE ASLEEP, **"THE DEAD IN CHRIST WILL RISE FIRST",** AND WE WHO ARE **"ALIVE"** (ON EARTH), AND REMAIN SHALL BE CAUGHT UP TO MEET THE LORD IN THE **"AIR",**

VERSE. 16

THE DEAD IN CHRIST, THOSE WHO HAVE DIED AND COME BACK WITH THE LORD; THEY SHALL BE WITH THEM IN THE **CLOUDS** (PEOPLE).

VERSE. 17

THE CHURCH **("SAINTS")** SHALL BE RAPTURED, AND ALL THE SAINTS THAT HAVE DIED IN THE LORD SHALL BE TOGETHER IN THE **CLOUDS** (PEOPLE), THE WORD **"CAUGHT UP"** GREEK WORD HARPAZO, WHICH MEANS, TO SNATCH UP.

VERSE. 18

COMFORT ONE ANOTHER, WE ARE TO WATCH, AND PRAY FOR ONE ANOTHER.

THE SECOND COMING OF CHRIST (CHAPTER 13)

AFTER THE ASCENSION JESUS'S PROMISE TO RETURN TO EARTH

THIS IS WHEN JESUS WAS TAKEN UP, AND HIS DISCIPLES SAW HIM (JESUS) NO MORE, FOR JESUS HAS GONE TO PREPARE A PLACE FOR THE SAINTS TO LIVE WITH HIM (JESUS) FOR EVER, AND EVER, AND JESUS IS COMING BACK AGAIN ONE DAY FOR A CHURCH WITHOUT SPOT OR WRINKLE, KEEP WATCHING AND PRAYING FOR ONE ANOTHER, THE LORD WILL COME BACK TO EARTH ONE DAY TO FIGHT THE BATTLE OF ARMAGEDDON, WHERE THE LORD WILL DESTROY THE

NATIONS WHO HAVE COME UP
AGAINST HIS PEOPLE TO
DESTROY (ANNIHILATION)
THEM UNDER THE BANNER OF
THE ANTICHRIST. TWO THIRDS
WILL ALREADY BE DEAD;
ONLY A THIRD WILL SURVIVE
WHEN THE LORD WILL STAND
ON THE MOUNT OF OLIVES IN
THAT DAY, THERE SHALL BE A
CHANGE IN THE SHAPE OF THE
LAND, THE RIVER WILL FLOW
ON BOTH SIDES OF THE BANKS
FOR HEALING, THE FRUIT FOR
MEAT, AND THE LEAVES FOR
MEDICINE.

THE LIGHTNING SHALL COME OUT OF THE EAST

THE SON OF MAN SHALL COME
FROM THE EAST, THE FOWL
SHALL FEAST ON THE BLOOD
OF MEN, ON THE MOUNTAIN OF
ISRAEL, AND AFTER THOSE
DAYS THE SUN SHALL BE

DARKING, THE MOON GIVING
NO LIGHT, ONLY DARKNESSS
OVER THE EARTH, AND THE
HEAVENS SHALL BE SHAKEN.
THE STARS SHALL FALL FROM
HEAVEN, IN THAT DAY THERE
WILL BE A RELIEF AND THE
SON OF MAN COMING IN THE
"CLOUDS" (PEOPLE); TO SET
THINGS IN ORDER AS THEY
SHOULD BE, MOVING TO THE
NEXT DISPENSATION: THE
COMING OF THE LORD AND THE
SAINTS AND ANGELS WITH HIM
(JESUS). THIS WILL BE A
GLORIOUS DAY WHEN JESUS
COMES BACK THE SECOND
TIME AS LORD OF LORDS, AND
KING OF KINGS. THERE SHALL
BE REJOICING IN THE LAND
AND NATIONS SHALL COME TO
WORSHIP THE KING. JESUS
WILL HAVE LAID DOWN ALL
AUTHORITY, MAN SHALL

LEARN HOW TO LIVE FOR GOD
AND BE AS ONE IN CHRIST. IT
WILL BE PEOPLE WHO NEED TO
BE SAVED, THIS IS DIFFERENT
FROM THE CHURCH, BUT WE
ALL SHALL BE ONE CHURCH
WHETHER YOU ARE A JEW OR
GENTILE. IT WILL NOT MATTER
WHAT NATIONALITY YOU ARE
IN CHRIST; WE WILL BE ONE AN
IN ALL WHO HAVE RECEIVED
HIS (JESUS') GRACE; JESUS
WILL GATHER HIS ELECT
(JEWS) FROM THE FOUR
CORNERS OF THE EARTH,
EVERY ONE WILL HAVE TO
ACCEPT JESUS AS LORD OF
LORDS, AND KING OF KINGS.

**HIS COMING WILL ALSO BE
VISIBLE (SEEN)**

JESUS IS COMING BACK IN THE
"CLOUDS" (PEOPLE),
EVERYONE ON THIS EARTH IS
GOING TO SEE JESUS WHEN

JESUS RETURNS THE SECOND
TIME; THEY THAT PIERCED HIM
(JEWS) SHALL WANT TO SEE
HIM (JESUS).

**ISRAEL WILL TURN TO HIM
(JESUS) WITH THEIR WHOLE
HEART**

FIRST THE LORD IS GOING TO
GATHER ALL THE **"NATIONS"**
THAT HAVE COME AGAINST
JERUSALEM, AND IN THAT DAY
JESUS WILL DESTROY ALL THE
NATIONS THAT HAS COME
AGAINST JERUSALEM TO FIGHT
AGAINST JERUSALEM TO
BATTLE **(ARMAGEDDON);**
THEY SHALL REPENT OF THEIR
SINS AND SHAME THAT THEY
HAVE BROUGHT ON THE LORD.
THEY WILL ACCEPT THAT
JESUS HAS BEEN RAISED FROM
THE DEAD, THAT HE LIVES AND
HE (JESUS) WANTS TO LIVE IN
THE LIVES OF MEN SO THEY

SHALL LIVE ALSO AND WILL BE DECLARED NOT GUILTY (PARDONED) FOR REJECTING THE MESSIAH.

FINAL SIEGE OF JERUSALEM, THE SUPER OF THE GREAT GOD

THE DAY OF THE LORD WILL COME, THE SECOND COMING OF THE LORD AND INTO THE MILLENIUM WHERE JESUS WILL REIGN AS LORD OF LORDS, AND KING OF KINGS, JESUS WIL PUT DOWN ALL RULE, AND AUTHORTY. JESUS WILL COMMAND THE FOWLS THAT WILL EAT ALL FLESH, THE BEAST , AND THE KINGS WILL GATHER TO MAKE WAR WITH CHRIST; BUT WILL BE DEFEATED BY CHRIST. THE BEAST, AND THE FALSE PROPHET SHALL BE CAST IN THE LAKE OF FIRE **(ALIVE),**

THEY SHALL NOT BE ABLE TO
DECEIVE **(MARK OF THE
BEAST),** THE NATIONS ANY
MORE. JESUS WILL HAVE
COMPLETE CONTROL OF THE
MILLENIUM PERIOD, WHICH
WILL LAST FOR A THOUSAND
YEARS,SATAN SHALL BE
BOUND FOR ONE THOUSAND
YEARS, AND AFTER THAT
SHALL BE LOOSE FOR A SHORT
TIME TO DO EVIL TO THE
"SAINTS." TO DECEIVE THEM
ONE MORE TIME, GOD SHALL
DEVOUR THEM **(SATAN ARMY
"PEOPLE")** FROM HEAVEN
WITH FIRE, THESE ARE THOSE
THAT REJECTED SALVATION,
AND THREW IN WITH SATAN TO
DESTROY THE SAINTS. SATAN'S
FOLLOWERS SHALL BE CAST IN
THE LAKE OF FIRE **("AFTER
THE GREAT WHITE THRONE
JUDGMENT")** FOR EVER AND

EVER, WHERE THE BEAST, AND THE FALSE PROPHET ARE. GOD GAVE THEM A CHANCE TO BE SAVED, BUT THEY REFUSED TO ACCEPT THE TRUTH TO LIVE WITH JESUS FOREVER. SATAN, HIS ANGELS AND THE SEDUCING SPIRITS SHALL ALSO BE CAST IN THE LAKE OF FIRE, WHERE THE BEAST, AND THE FALSE PROPHET ARE. ALL EVIL WILL BE DESTROYED, **"DEATH IS THE LAST THING"**, THIS IS WHAT CHRIST HAS DONE FOR THE SAINTS **"HALLELUJAH"**

FUTURE JUDGMENT OF FALSE TEACHERS

ENOCH PROPHESIED THESE SAYING TO EXCUTE JUDGMENT UPON THE FALSE TEACHERS IN THESE LAST DAYS, ALL WILL BE JUDGED FOR THEIR SPEECH, AND

HARD WORDS AGAINST GOD, AND HIS PEOPLE, CHRIST WILL ADDRESS THESE ISSUES FROM FRONT TO BACK; THE FALSE DOCTRINES, THE APOSTASY OF THE CHURCH, AND IT'S ENTIRETY. THIS WILL BE A TIME OF THE DAM, FOR THEY SHALL CALL ON HIM (JESUS) WHOM THEY HAVE NOT BELIEVED IN, AND CALL ON JESUS NAME TO BE SAVED, IN WHOM THEY HAVE NOT BELIEVED. THEIR METHODS WERE DISHONEST; LYING CHEATING, AND STEALING. TO SAY THE LEAST OF THE EFFORT THAT THEY HAVE PUT IN THE CHURCH. THE THING THAT WILL DESTROY SOUND DOCTRINE IS NOT HAVING THE RIGHT

171

WORDS, NOR THE RIGHT PEOPLE
WHO HAVE THE SPIRIT OF
CHRIST. ALWAYS GRUMBLING,
NEVER BEING CONTENT WITH
WHAT YOU HAVE. WANTING
MORE THAN YOU CAN BARE.
THESE ARE FALSE WITNESSES
THAT WILL NOT TELL THE
TRUTH, BECAUSE THE SPIRIT OF
TRUTH IS NOT IN THEM, FOR
THEY HAVE NO CONSCIOUS OF
WHAT THEY DO. **"THE
SUDUCING SPIRITS"** HAVE
TAKEN OVER THEIR LIVES, THEY
HAVE BEEN TURNED OVER TO A
"REPROBATE MIND", MEANING
WORTHLESSNESS, GOOD FOR
NOTHING OR NEVER COMING
TO THE KNOWLEDGE OF THE
TRUTH. IF YOU LOOK AROUND

YOU TODAY YOU WILL SEE
THEM, PEOPLE HAVE GOTTEN
TO WHERE RIGHT IS WRONG,
AND WRONG IS RIGHT, THEIR
MIND IS ALL TWISTED UP, THEY
KNOW NOT WHICH WAY TO GO.
THEY ARE LED BY A FALSE SENSE
OF SECURITY AND THEY ARE
LEADING OTHERS DOWN THE
WRONG PATH. PEOPLE JUST
WANT TO BELONG TO
SOMETHING, IT SEEMS TO
REPLACE THAT VOID THAT IS IN
THEIR HEARTS; THEY WANT TO
BECOME WHAT THEY CAN'T BE,
SO THEY ACT IT OUT AND THEY
HOPE THAT IT WILL BE ENOUGH
TO GET TO THE NEXT FIX. IT ALL
ACTS LIKE A DRUG THAT'S THE
WAY LIFE IS WITHOUT CHRIST

("CROSS"). THERE IS NO OTHER WAY OUT BUT THE CROSS. DO NOT LISTEN TO THESE FALSE TEACHERS; THEY ARE FULL OF LIES, DECEPTION, FALSE PROMISES, MISLEADING INFORMATION, FLATTERY, ETC...,. THEY SHALL COME IN THE NAME OF CHRIST, BUT DO NOT BELIEVE THEM FOR THEY ARE LIKE A ROARING LION, SEEKING PREY AND THEY SHALL DECEIVE MANY BECAUSE THEY HAVE NOT THE SPIRIT OF CHRIST. IF YOU ARE GOING TO BE ABLE TO STAND, YOU WILL HAVE TO PUT THE WHOLE ARMOUR OF GOD ON AND THAT IS **"EVERY WORD"** THAT PROCEEDETH OUT OF THE

MOUTH OF GOD, THE WORLD
WILL HATE YOU BECAUSE OF
CHRIST, THEY FIRST HATED. IF
THEY HATED CHRIST THEY WILL
ALSO HATE YOU. MANY PEOPLE
HAVE BEEN DECEIVED BY THESE
FALSE TEACHERS, THEY ARE
EVERY WHERE THE TRUTH IS
BEING TAUGHT. THEIR JOB IS TO
DISRUPT THE PROCESS, SO YOU
WILL REJECT OR DENOUNCE
CHRIST, FOR PEOPLE ARE
SERVING WORKS INSTEAD OF
THE LIVING GOD. WHAT I AM
SAYING: YOU CAN'T HAVE THE
SPIRIT WITHOUT THE BODY, YOU
CAN'T HAVE FAITH WITHOUT
THE WORKS, EVERYTHING
WORKS TOGETHER AS ONE
SPIRIT. THESE FALSE TEACHERS

WHO ARE LEADING YOU
WITHOUT THE SPIRIT OF CHRIST;
THERE IS NO OTHER WAY BUT
CHRIST AND HIM **(JESUS)**
CRUCIFIED. STAY AWAY FROM
FALSE TEACHING; IT WILL ONLY
LED YOU FURTHER IN DARKNESS,
A PLACE YOU WILL NOT WANT
TO BE, WAKE UP FROM THE
DEAD AND LIVE. ASK CHRIST TO
COME IN YOUR LIFE TO BE YOUR
SAVIOR, JESUS, WANTS TO BE
LORD OF YOUR LIFE AND TO
BRING YOU OUT OF BONDAGE
TO BE WITH HIM (JESUS).

THE JUDGMENT OF THE NATIONS (GENTILES)

THIS WILL HAPPEN AFTER THE
SECOND COMING OR DURING
THE SECOND COMING OF

CHRIST. WHEN CHRIST WILL SIT
UPON HIS THRONE, AND
GATHER THE NATIONS
TOGETHER TO SEPARATE THE
GOOD **(SHEEP),** AND THE BAD
(GOATS), THOSE THAT WILL BE
WITH CHRIST, AND THOSE
THAT WILL BE CAST INTO
EVERLASTING FIRE TO BE WITH
THEIR FATHER (DEVIL). THERE
WILL NOT BE A SECOND
CHANCE TO SAY WAIT
BECAUSE YOU HAVE REJECTED
SALVATION WHEN IT WAS
OFFERED TO YOU. **"YOU SAY
WHAT HAVE WE REJECTED?"**
YOUR BROTHERS AND
SISTERS;YOU MAY SAY I DON'T
HAVE ANY BROTHERS OR
SISTERS. LET'S UNDERSTAND
SOMETHING, WHAT YOU DO TO
OTHERS YOU DO UNTO THE
LORD. WHEN WE TALK ABOUT
OTHERS WE ARE TALKING

ABOUT THE LORD, WHEN WE
STEAL FROM OTHERS WE
STEAL FROM THE LORD. OUR
NEIGHBOR IS NOT JUST NEXT
DOOR OR ACROSS THE STREET,
BUT EVERY WHERE; ALL OVER
THE WORLD. IF WE LOVE ONLY
THOSE WHO LOVE US, WE ARE
NOT DOING ANYTHING. WE
MUST LOVE THOSE WHO HATE
US AND DESPITEFULY USE US.
IF YOU LOOK AT THE COLOR OF
A PERSON'S SKIN YOU ARE
GOING TO MISS THE MARK.
(SIN) WITHOUT THE LOVE OF
CHRIST YOU WILL NOT BE ABLE
TO LOVE YOUR ENEMIES. IT
TAKES THE SPIRIT OF CHRIST
TO FULFILL THIS TASK AND
THAT IS IN EVERYTHING WE DO
FOR CHRIST. YOU CAN'T DO
THIS ON YOUR OWN; YOU NEED
THE SPIRIT TO TALK, WALK
WITH YOU AND GUIDE YOU IN

THE RIGHT DIRECTION. **"I SAY THIS AGAIN"** YOU CAN'T DO THIS ON YOUR OWN, YOU NEED THE SPIRIT TO TALK WITH YOU, WALK WITH YOU, AND GUIDE YOU IN THE RIGHT DIRECTION. IT IS CHRIST WHO KEEPS US AND NOT OURSELVES. WE ARE BOUGHT WITH A PRICE; WE ARE LED TO THE SLAUGHTER ALL THE DAY LONG, OUR TRUST MUST BE IN CHRIST AND NOTHING ELSE. WE CAN'T LOVE GOD AND HATE OUR BROTHER WHOM WE WALK DAILY WITH; WE MUST LOVE ONE ANOTHER, FOR CHRIST HAS COMMANDED THAT WE LOVE ONE ANOTHER AS CHRIST HAS LOVED THE CHURCH. GOD GAVE HIS ONLY SON (JESUS) THAT WE MAY HAVE **"EVERLASTING LIFE."** THAT WE MAY LIVE WITH CHRIST

FOREVER AND EVER, FOR WE
ARE FREE MEN FOR THOSE
WHO HAVE BELIEVED IN THE
SON OF GOD. WE ARE NOT IN
BONDAGE TO ANY MAN, SO LET
US WALK IN NEWNESS WITH
ONE ANOTHER. THAT WE MAY
PLEASE THE FATHER WHICH
ARE IN HEAVEN. THE GOD OF
THE UNIVERSE, WHO DWELLS
IN ALL MEN; WHO PUT THEIR
TRUST IN THE SAVIOR. IF GOD
IS IN US, WE MUST LEARN TO
LOVE OUR BROTHER THE WAY
CHRIST LOVES US. YOU MUST
GIVE YOUR HEART **"(BELIEVE)"**
TO JESUS AND WHAT WE DO TO
OUR BROTHER IS WHAT WE DO
TO CHRIST. YOU CAN'T LOVE
GOD JUST ON SUNDAY
MORNINGS, WEDNESDAYS OR
ANY DAY OF THE WEEK; YOU
MUST LOVE WHEN IT IS NOT
CONVENIENT FOR YOU TO

LOVE. WE CAN'T PICK AND
CHOOSE THE FRIENDS WE
LOVE; WE MUST SHOW LOVE
AT ALL TIMES AND HUMBLE
OURSELVES AS LITTLE
CHILDREN, IF WE ARE GOING
TO SEE GOD. **"LIVE WITH GOD
FOREVER AND EVER."** DON'T
GAIN THIS WHOLE WORLD,
LIKE SO MANY THAT HAVE
LOST THEIR SOUL FOR WHAT
DID NOT BELONG TO THEM.
SATAN HAD TRICKED AND
DECEIVED SO MANY PEOPLE IN
TO THINKING THAT HE STILL
HAS THE **"KEYS TO HELL",**
THAT IS A LIE, JESUS MADE IT
ALL POSSIBLE AT THE CROSS
WHEN HE DIED FOR ALL MAN
KIND. **"FOR JESUS HAS THE
KEYS TO HELL AND DEATH."**
SATAN HAS LOST HIS POWER
THAT HE (SATAN) HAD IN THIS
WORLD, THAT KEPT MAN IN

BONDAGE, JESUS HAS
"REDEEMED" MAN BACK TO
GOD; ALL YOU HAVE TO DO IS
PUT YOUR **"FAITH"** IN CHRIST
AND THOU (YOU) SHALL BE
SAVED. **"NO ONE"** WILL
ESCAPE FROM THE **"WRATH"**
OF GOD, WORLD WITHOUT END.

THE GREAT WHITE THRONE JUDGMENT

MAN WILL STAND BEFORE GOD
TO BE JUDGE, THIS WILL TAKE
PLACE AT THE **"GREAT WHITE
THRONE."** THIS WILL BE THE
JUDGMENT OF THEM **"THE
WICKED"** WHOSE NAME IS NOT
WRITTEN IN THE LAMB'S BOOK
OF LIFE, THERE IS NO REWARD
FOR THOSE WHOSE NAMES ARE
NOT WRITTEN IN THE BOOK OF
LIFE, THEY WILL BE JUDGED BY
THEIR **"WORKS."** THIS IS THE
SECOND DEATH, THESE PEOPLE
WILL NOT REIGN WITH CHRIST;

THEY SHALL BE CAST IN THE
"LAKE OF FIRE" BECAUSE
THEY REJECTED CHRIST
"CROSS." THAT THEY MIGHT
BE SAVED. EVERY MAN HAD
THE CHANCE TO BE WITH
CHRIST, THEY CHOSE TO LIVE
"NOT BY FAITH," THAT JESUS
WOULD SAVE THEM. SATAN,
HIS ARMY (A THIRD), THE ANTI-
CHRIST, FALSE PROPHET, AND
THE DEMON SPIRITS; THEY
WILL NOT BE JUDGED THE
SAME AS MAN BECAUSE THEY
HAVE ALREADY BEEN
CONDEMNED BY GOD. ALL
WILL HAVE THEIR PART IN THE
LAKE OF FIRE, THERE WILL BE
TWO BOOKS FOR THE PEOPLE
("MAN"); ONE WILL BE THE
WORKS MAN HAS DONE IN THIS
LIFE, AND THE BOOK OF LIFE
WILL DETERMINE IF HE OR SHE
WILL GET IN HEAVEN. THE

TRUTH IS MAN WILL NOT MAKE
IT IN HEAVEN BECAUSE THE
GREAT WHITE THRONE IS THE
JUDGMENT OF GOD AGAINST
MAN, FOR THE SINS THAT MAN
NEVER REPENTED OF. NO SIN
WILL ENTER HEAVEN, IF THE
BLOOD **"JESUS CHRIST"** DOES
NOT COVER YOU, THE LAKE OF
FIRE WILL BE YOUR HOME FOR
"ETERNITY." THE **"SECOND
DEATH"** HAS NO POWER,
TODAY IS THE DAY OF
SALVATION WHILE THE BLOOD
RUNS WARM IN YOUR VEINS.
WHEN WILL THIS JUDGMENT
TAKE PLACE? RIGHT AFTER
THE EARTH, AND THE HEAVEN
ARE FLED AWAY. THIS IS AFTER
THE **"MILLENNIAL,"** WHEN
ALL SIN WILL BE NO MORE.
THIS WILL BE THE FINAL
JUDGMENT OF MAN, WE WILL
ALL BE ON ONE ACCORD WITH

EACH OTHER, SERVING GOD
DAY AND NIGHT. THEIR WILL
BE NATURAL PEOPLE
**("WITHOUT GLORIFIED
BODIES")** LIVING; THEY WILL
BE HEALED BY THE TREES
THAT EZEKIEL TALKS ABOUT
IN

EZEKIEL 47:12 And by the river upon the
bank thereof, on this side and on that side, shall
grow all trees for meat, whose leaf shall not
fade, neither shall the fruit thereof be consumed:
it shall bring forth new fruit according to his
months, because their waters they issued out of
the sanctuary: and the fruit thereof shall be for
meat, and the leaf thereof for medicine.

THEY WILL LIVE FOREVER IN
THIS STATE BECAUSE THEY
WERE NOT RAPTURED WITH
THE CHURCH, ONLY THE ONE'S
WHO DIED BEFORE THE
RAPTURE, AND THE
TRIBULATION SAINTS WILL
HAVE **"GLORIED BODIES"**
FOREVER. THE REST OF THE

PEOPLE **("THOSE WHO ARE SAVED")** WILL BE HEALED BY THE TREES THAT BRING FORTH MEAT **("FRUIT"),** AND THE LEAF **("MEDICINE");** THIS WILL TAKE CARE OF THEM FROM MONTH TO MONTH, THIS WILL BE ONE CHURCH REGARDLESS OF THE CONDITION OF THE PEOPLE. THIS IS THE SAME THING AS THE DEGREES PEOPLE THAT ARE IN THE LAKE OF FIRE, OR WERE IN HELL WILL EXPERIENCE. OR THE REWARDS THAT PEOPLE WILL RECEIVE, EVERY MAN WILL BE BLESSED ACCORDING TO **("DEEDS"),** SO IT MAKES A BIG DIFFERENCE IN THIS LIFE THE WAY YOU LIVE FOR CHRIST, REMEMBER NO SIN WILL ENTER IN THE KINGDOM OF HEAVEN, **ONLY THE "PURE IN SPIRIT"** WILL SEE GOD.

THE END OF THE TRIBULATION PERIOD IS WHEN JESUS WILL COME BACK

THE TRIBULATION PERIOD WILL LAST FOR SEVEN YEARS, (THREE AND A HALF YEARS OF **"PEACE",** AND THREE AND A HALF YEARS OF **"TROUBLE").** THAT MAN HAS NEVER KNOWN, OR WILL BE ABLE TO WITH STAND, FOR THIS WILL BE A TIME OF **"JACOB'S TROUBLE."** A TIME THAT NO MAN WILL BE ABLE TO STAND WITHOUT THE PEACE OF CHRIST THAT DWELL WITH IN THE HEART OF MAN. THEIR WILL BE WARS, EARTHQUAKES, NO PEACE ON THE EARTH, FAMINE WILL BE IN THE LAND, DEATH, AND HUNGER SHALL BE IN THE LAND. THE LAND WILL BE CHANGED; WINTER, SUMMER,

FALL AND SPRING WILL BE
DIFFERENT IN CLIMATE. IT
WILL EFFECT EVERY THING IN
THE LAND, THIS IS A SCARY
MOMENT BECAUSE MAN WILL
HAVE NO CONTROL OF THE
SITUATION. HE WILL NOT EVEN
BE ABLE TO GET OUT OF THE
WAY OF THE TROUBLE THAT IS
COMING UPON THE EARTH, THE
NEWS WILL HAVE NO CONTROL
OF GOD'S PLAN. THE LEADERS
OF THE WORLD WILL BE
HELPLESS, THEY WILL RUN FOR
COVER, THEY WILL NOT BE
ABLE TO HELP THE PEOPLE.
EVERYONE IS GOING TO
EXPERIENCE THIS
TRIBULATION THAT IS LEFT
BACK ON THIS EARTH AFTER
THE RAPTURE, NO ONE KNOWS
WHEN THE TRIBULATION WILL
START **("IT WILL START WHEN
ISRAEL SIGN THE PEACE**

TREATY"). THE ANTI-CHRIST WILL PRETEND TO LOVE HIS FELLOW MAN UNTIL THE THREE AND A HALF YEARS ARE UP. BEFORE THE END OF THE THREE AND A HALF YEARS, THE ANTI-CHRIST WILL SHOW HIS TRUE COLORS, THEN WILL ALL HELL BREAK OUT. THE ANTI-CHRIST TRUE COLORS WILL BE REVEALED FOR THE FIRST TIME. ISRAEL WILL KNOW THAT THEY HAVE BEEN **"DECEIVED"** IN BELIEVING A LIE FOR THREE AND A HALF YEARS AND THERE WILL BE A HUNDRED AND FORTY AND FOUR THOUSAND SERVANTS SEALED; TWELVE THOUSAND OUT OF EACH TRIBE THAT WILL WITNESS FOR GOD, THESE ARE THE SERVANTS JESUS HAS PREPARED FOR THE DAY IN WHICH HE **("JESUS")** WILL

GUIDE AND DIRECT THEM BY
THE SPIRIT. GOD'S NAME WILL
BE WRITTEN IN THEIR
"FOREHEADS" AND THESE
SERVANTS ARE **"JEWS."** LET NO
ONE DECEIVE YOU, THESE ARE
NOT GENTILES OR PART OF THE
CHURCH, NOR THE
TRIBULATION SAINTS; THE
BIBLE PLAINLY TELLS US IN
REVELATION, THE SEVENTH
CHAPTER, VERSE FOUR THAT
THESE ARE THE **"CHILDREN OF
ISRAEL."** THEY HAVE BEEN
REDEEMED FROM THE EARTH,
AND WITHOUT FAULT BEFORE
THE THRONE OF GOD. THEY
HAVE A SPECIAL ASSIGNMENT;
NOT JUST ANY MAN WILL BE
ABLE TO DO THE WORK GOD
HAS FOR THESE SERVANTS.
YOU MUST BE
"REDEEMED"AND WITHOUT
FAULT. THIS DESCRIPTION

DOES NOT FIT ANY MAN THAT DID NOT GO IN THE RAPTURE OR WERE LEFT BEHIND, THE SEA WILL BE TURNED INTO BLOOD, A GREAT STAR **"WORMWOOD"** WILL FALL FROM HEAVEN. THE PEOPLE WILL DEAL WITH A THIRD PART IN THE LAND, SEAS, RIVERS, MOON, STARS, AND SUN. THIS WILL BRING DEATH OVER THE EARTH; THIS IS **"GOD'S JUDGEMENT"** ON MAN TO BRING MAN TO REPENTANCE, SO THAT HIS SOUL CAN BE SAVED FROM HELL; THAT MAN WILL NOT END UP IN THE LAKE OF FIRE. THERE ARE GOING TO BE MEN WHO WILL WANT TO DIE BUT CAN'T, BECAUSE GOD IS IN CONTROL OF MAN'S LIFE, AND MAN IS NOT IN CONTROL OF HIS OWN LIFE, THERE IS NO NEUTRAL GROUND FOR DEATH;

WHEN YOU DIE, YOUR SOUL
STILL LIVES ON FOREVER.
BELIEVE NOT THE LIE THAT
SATAN HAS TOLD YOU, THAT
WHEN YOU DIE YOU'RE DEAD.
THAT IS A LIE FROM THE PITS
OF HELL, GAIN KNOWLEDGE
AND LIVE FOR GOD. GOD'S
WORD WILL NOT COME BACK
TO HIM **"GOD"** VOID; THE
WORD OF GOD IS TRUE. THE
SON OF MAN **"JESUS CHRIST"**
IS COMING BACK TO THE
EARTH ONE DAY AND VERY
SOON. WILL YOU BE
"READY"TO COME BACK WITH
HIM **"JESUS"** FROM HEAVEN?
ONLY THE BODY IS IN THE
GRAVE, THE SOUL AND SPIRIT
IS WITH GOD. THERE WILL BE A
FALLEN AWAY FIRST, MEANING
THE RAPTURE WILL TAKE
PLACE FIRST; THEN THE ANTI-
CHRIST MUST COME FIRST

BEFORE THE SECOND COMING
OF CHRIST WILL TAKE PLACE
ON THE EARTH. THE ANTI-
CHRIST WILL ONLY CONTROL A
CERTAIN PORTION OF THE
EARTH; HE WILL ALSO HAVE
WORSHIPPERS UPON THE
EARTH TO WORSHIP THE IMAGE
OF THE BEAST. THIS WILL TAKE
PLACE DURING THE SECOND
HALF OF THE TRIBULATION
PERIOD. SOME PEOPLE WILL
BELIEVE A LIE; FOR THE TRUTH
WILL NOT BE IN THEM. THIS IS
HAPPENING TODAY THAT SOME
PEOPLE WILL RATHER BELIEVE
OR TELL A LIE, THAN FACE THE
TRUTH AND BE SET FREE FROM
BONDAGE; AND LIVE FOR
CHRIST. PLAGUES SHALL BE
FIRE, SMOKE, AND BRIMSTONE
TO HURT MAN KIND; GOD
SHALL SEND HIS TWO
WITNESSES TO PROPHECY

FORTY- TWO MONTHS **("360 DAYS * 3 YEARS = 1080 DAYS + ½ OF 360 DAYS = 180 DAYS WHICH 1080 + 180 DAYS = 1260 DAYS")** THIS IS HOW WE GET THE PROPHECY OF THE TWO WITNESSES. THE JEWS USED 360 DAYS INSTEAD OF 365 DAYS THAT WE USE TODAY; THE TWO WITNESSES HAD POWER TO SHUT HEAVEN, TO TURN WATER IN TO BLOOD, AND SMITE THE EARTH WITH PLAGUES, THEY WILL NOT BE KILLED UNTIL THEY HAVE FINISHED THEIR TESTIMONY AND THEIR BODIES SHALL LIE IN THE STREET THREE AND A HALF DAYS. THE PEOPLE SHALL REJOICE THAT THEY ARE DEAD, BUT AFTER THREE DAYS AN A HALF, THE SPIRIT OF GOD SHALL REVIVE **("LIFE")** INTO THEM AGAIN, ONLY THE

REMNANT WAS AFRAID AND
GAVE GLORY TO GO. SATAN
AND HIS ANGELS WILL BE CAST
OUT OF HEAVEN FOREVER;
THEY WILL NOT HAVE ACCESS
TO VISIT ANYMORE AND
SATAN WILL NOT BE ABLE TO
"ACCUSE" THE BRETHREN
EITHER. SATAN WILL WORK
FAST TO DECEIVE THE PEOPLE
IN THE EARTH BECAUSE SATAN
WILL ONLY HAVE JUST A
SHORT TIME AND HE WILL TRY
TO DECEIVE AS MANY AS HE
(SATAN) CAN. MEN WILL FAINT
FOR THE LACK OF FAITH,
DEATH, AND FEAR OF DYING.
SOME WILL EVEN FOLLOW
SATAN AND WILL TAKE THE
MARK OF THE BEAST. THERE
CAN'T AND WILL NOT BE ANY
"PARDONS" FOR ANY MAN
WHO TAKES THE MARK OF THE
BEAST; THE **"CROSS"** WILL NOT

COVER THE MARK OF THE BEAST. YOUR CHURCH WILL NOT GET YOU TO HEAVEN, YOUR MEMBERSHIP WILL NOT GET YOU TO HEAVEN, THE ONLY THING THAT WILL HELP YOU IS **"JESUS CHRIST AND HIM CRUCIFIED."** THERE IS NO OTHER ANSWER, BUT **"THE CROSS OF JESUS."** MAKE HIM (JESUS) LORD OF YOUR LIFE **("SURRENDER")** AND LIVE FOREVER AND EVER WITH CHRIST.

I THANK YOU FOR TAKING TIME TO ALLOW GOD TO SPEAK TO YOUR HEART, AND TO MAKE HIS PRESENCE KNOWN TO YOU, I PRAY THAT YOU WILL RECEIVE HIS (JESUS) SPIRIT AND HIS (JESUS) GUIDING LIGHT; LET JESUS LEAD YOU IN JESUS NAME. AMEN, AMEN.

Made in the USA
Columbia, SC
15 October 2021